CW00472491

Rock around the Peak
Megalithic Monuments
of the Peak District

Victoria & Paul Morgan

SIGMA
Leisure

Copyright © Victoria B. Morgan & Paul E. Morgan, 2001

All Rights Reserved. No part of this publication may be reproduced, stored in a retrieval system, or transmitted in any form or by any means – electronic, mechanical, photocopying, recording, or otherwise – without prior written permission from the publisher or a licence permitting restricted copying issued by the Copyright Licensing Agency, 90 Tottenham Court Road, London W1P 0LA. This book may not be lent, resold, hired out or otherwise disposed of by trade in any form of binding or cover other than that in which it is published, without the prior consent of the publisher.

Published by Sigma Leisure – an imprint of
Sigma Press, 1 South Oak Lane, Wilmslow, Cheshire SK9 6AR, England.

British Library Cataloguing in Publication Data
A CIP record for this book is available from the British Library.

ISBN: 1-85058-742-6

Cover photograph: Five Wells Chambered Cairn, Taddington Moor, Derbyshire

Maps and illustrations: Paul & Vicky Morgan

Typesetting and Design by: Sigma Press, Wilmslow, Cheshire.

Cover design: Design House, Marple Bridge

Printed by: MFP Design and Print

Disclaimer: the information in this book is given in good faith and is believed to be correct at the time of publication. No responsibility is accepted by either the author or publisher for errors or omissions, or for any loss or injury howsoever caused. Only you can judge your own fitness, competence and experience.

Preface

In January 1999, we made a New Year resolution to visit the ancient sites which were almost on our doorstep, but which for years we had never really taken time to discover. Upon examining maps and books it soon became apparent that there was no one positive source which covered all the prehistoric monuments in the Peak District. There were a number of websites that came close, yet even with today's technological advances it is still almost impossible to take these out into the field. As a result we decided to compile our own definitive guide, which seemed the perfect way of combining our disciplines of history, geology and the environment.

The aim of this book, therefore, is to provide a guide to all the prehistoric sites of note, in and around the Peak District of Derbyshire, with details of how to find them and a little bit of background as to their history and construction. We do not go into great archaeological detail about each site as there are many good books on this subject already and everyone has their own theories. However we have incorporated the five major types of ancient archaeological features to be found in the region – henges, stone circles, burial monuments, prehistoric rock art and hillforts. A glossary of terms can be found at the back of the book.

Being parents ourselves we have written this book with regard to family outings, describing the quickest and easiest route to each monument. Many of the sites listed can, of course, be incorporated into longer walks for those uninhibited by young children or those with an enthusiasm for rambles.

We made use of the shorter routes, as the majority of sites were visited with our lively toddler in tow (and latterly her baby sister). The stone circles of Derbyshire are amongst her favourites, possibly because they are comparatively small in size, making them perfect for young children to enjoy.

Whatever your reasons for visiting these ancient places, we hope you will appreciate them as much as we do.

Paul & Vicky Morgan

Acknowledgements

Our thanks go to the many professional and amateur archaeologists and historians whose works originally pointed us in the direction of these ancient sites, particularly John Barnatt, Senior Survey Archaeologist for the Peak District National Park Authority and Alastair McIvor, developer of the superb Derbyshire stone circle website.

We are also very grateful to John Bishop, Estates Service Manager, and Ken Smith, Archaeological Service Manager, of the Peak District National Park Authority for granting us permission to visit the Barbrook stone circles in the Sanctuary Area of the Eastern Moors Estate. Our thanks also goes to Ros Westwood of the Buxton Museum for providing us with the photograph of the Bronze Age urns from Stanton Moor (page 98) and Dave Martin, Chief Flying Instructor at the Derbyshire and Lancashire Gliding Club, for the aerial photograph of Burr Tor hillfort (page 142).

Thanks also to both our mothers: Vicky's – Dorothy Bentley Smith – for advice on the text and Paul's – Judy Webb – for allowing us to use her photographs of Arbor Low (page 17), and Doll Tor (page 76).

Finally, we would like to say a very big 'thank you' to our eldest daughter Megan who happily spent her holidays and weekends wandering all over the countryside and visiting the ancient sites; and latterly her baby sister Charlotte.

For our Sun Baby, Megan
and
our Millennium Baby, Charlotte

Contents

Introduction

The British Isles is home to some of the earliest surviving man-made structures in the world. The first Neolithic monuments were constructed some 500 years before the Great Pyramids of Egypt (2575BC to 2465BC), while the Late Bronze Age and Early Iron Age hillforts are roughly contemporary with the Olmec Temples of Central America (1150BC to 400BC).

Our small islands contain a myriad of ancient monuments, many fine examples of which are located in the Peak District. In order to try to gain a deeper understanding as to their purpose, we first need to look at the people who constructed them and the environment of the time.

The ancient landscape and its people

Throughout prehistory ancient man was inextricably drawn to rocks and stone. He skilfully shaped them to make tools and weapons, used large blocks of them to create special monuments and carved ring, spiral and zigzag designs into their surface, but for what purpose we are not sure. With its breathtaking heights, rocky hilltops, rugged crags and stunning tors the Peak District is, by nature, the epitome of everything stone. Even today, the symbol of the Peak National Park is a millstone (a stone circle!).

Lying at the southern end of the Pennines, the Peak District lies largely within Britain's first and most popular National Park and is divided into two distinct regions; the central lowland limestone plateau of the White Peak and the surrounding upland millstone grit areas of the Dark Peak. Separating the two are highly fertile valleys cut into the softer shale bedrock.

The first farmers

Until the Neolithic period ancient man was a hunter-gatherer. He lived a nomadic lifestyle and was reliant on whatever food and shelter nature provided. During the 'New Stone Age', sometime between 4500BC and 2500BC, a social transformation took place and the British Isles saw the advent of the first farmers. At this time, the Peak District was particularly attractive for settlement. With its rich soils and abundance of fresh water, it provided the ideal location for both arable and pastoral farming.

Apart from the highest areas, where peat was beginning to form, both the limestone plateau and the gritstone uplands were highly fertile regions. The White Peak was dominated by areas of ash woodland interspersed with pasture, while the Dark Peak was composed of oak and birch, again broken by open areas of grassland. Only the valleys themselves were densely forested.

   The most fertile regions were the shelves on either side of the river valleys, between the limestone plateau and the gritstone uplands and it was
here that permanent colonisation initially occurred. For the first time in
history man began to cultivate his own crops and breed his own livestock,
on a small scale at first, but nevertheless reshaping the landscape as he did
so. Without the constant need to search for food and shelter, Neolithic man
had stability and time on his hands. With farming came the accumulation
of 'wealth' and resources, and a population that looked beyond one human
lifespan. Early man was now able to work in unison with his fellow farmers
to create large-scale ritual monuments, the likes of which had never been
seen before. Constructed as investments for the future, these sites developed as a territorial focus, designed to impress.

   All of the early Peak monuments are located on the limestone plateau.
Although the early farmers first settled in the sheltered river valleys, they
almost certainly used the limestone plateau and upland areas for seasonal
grazing, but there is no evidence to suggest there was permanent settlement
here. They perhaps visited pastures on higher ground in the warmer
months, but returned to a lowland 'base' during the colder seasons.

   The huge Neolithic monuments such as the henges were created near
the best grazing areas on the limestone plateau where the mobile farming
groups were most likely to meet, perhaps reinforcing traditional claims to
the pasture. Others such as burial chambers and barrows were placed close
to the well-used pathways between the various regions. For the first time in
the history of mankind, permanent man-made features were erected which
would far outlast the people who created them.

   Another consequence of farming was that more tools were required to
clear the land and construct dwellings and ritual monuments. Living in a
time before metal was discovered, these early settlers used stone tools such
as knives, scrapers, borers and flint arrowheads, many of which have been
discovered in all three regions of the Peak District. For over 2000 years,
stone was the primary raw material. This in turn led to the large-scale
mining of flint and quarrying of stone. Axe production was at its peak. At
Grimes Graves mines in Norfolk alone, it has been estimated that from the
five hundred shafts mined over five hundred years, some five million axes
could have been produced (Mercer, 1998).

   Particularly prized were highly polished axes made from special hard
stone. Over one hundred of these have been discovered in the Peak District,
originating from as far away as axe factories in Northern Ireland, the Lake
District and North Wales. However, such axes appear to have been revered
for their mystical properties rather than used for practical application. The
ritual significance of the axe is particularly evident at Stonehenge where
several of the stones have axes and daggers carved into them.

A stone axe head

The trade of such prestige items accelerated during the Later Neolithic period and by circa 2500BC, simple exchange had given way to major complex trading networks. Research in the British Isles has shown that items such as axes were transported along well-established trade routes and exchanged at certain 'safe' peripheral locations or staging posts. This increase in trade coincides almost exactly with the construction of the henge monuments and it has been suggested that the two large Derbyshire henges, Arbor Low and the Bull Ring at Dove Holes, may well have been places where such transactions occurred.

Archaeologists have completed excavations on Gardom's Edge, the large shelf of land above Baslow, which once lay on the main route from the Peak in the west to the flint rich areas of Yorkshire and Lincolnshire in the east. They discovered a large enclosure dating to the Neolithic period (see the *Rock Art* section for further details). Such large hilltop sites, defended by bank and ditch were common in the south of England in the Earlier Neolithic. The most famous example being Windmill Hill in Wiltshire.

Composed of a low, wide rubble bank over 600 metres long, the Gardom's Edge enclosure has seven entrances. As there appears to be no evidence for occupation here and Neolithic flint artefacts such as arrowheads and polished flint axes have been discovered nearby, archaeologists believe that the enclosure may also have been an important centre for trade.

Although these henges and enclosures are highly impressive and would have taken a large degree of communal co-operation, they are very rare. The most common monuments from this period are the chambered cairns and long barrows, built on a local level by smaller kin and family groups for ritual purposes

Essentially built as funerary monuments, they were not however burial chambers in the sense we know them today. Evidence suggests that they were special places where the bones of the dead were stored, brought out periodically, perhaps for important rituals and ceremonies. We know that they were not just graves, as quite often only select bones, such as the skull and the long bones of the arms and legs, not whole skeletons, were placed in these chambers.

The circle builders

In the British Isles in general, after around 2500BC, it is clear that power was becoming more centralised and farming populations were joining to form large tribal groupings. Leaders were starting to emerge and with this political power came increased trade links. Exotic goods were sought from abroad, in particular finely decorated pottery vessels, known to archaeologists as 'Beakers'. However, the most important discovery at this time was the importation of metal technology. The first copper and gold objects came to Britain closely followed by those who knew where and how to find the ore.

Although metal was now obtainable, it would not really have affected the average man in the field. Metal tools, like the polished stone axes before them, were seen as prestigious goods and appear largely in the burial deposits and round barrows of the elite. Farmers would have continued to use stone and flint on a day to day basis. During this metal revolution, Britain held a very strong position as one of the very few places in Europe where tin (combined with copper to make bronze) was readily available.

Around 1700BC, the population had undergone a massive expansion, supported by farming; wealth was becoming more widely distributed and bronze tools were reaching places far and wide. The extent of farming must have been considerable, encompassing massive tracts of land on a scale that has hardly been seen since.

Following considerable research in the Peak District, it has now been established that by the Bronze Age (circa 2000BC to 1500BC), agricultural communities of kin and family groups began to find permanent settlement on the limestone plateau and the lower slopes of the fertile gritstone uplands. Of particular interest are the Eastern Moors above the Derwent and Hope valleys, since it is here that the majority of the circles were constructed (Barnatt & Smith, 1997, Barnatt 1999).

Described by John Barnatt, Senior Survey Archaeologist for the Peak District National Park Authority, as 'one of the best preserved Bronze Age landscapes in Britain' it is hard to believe today that these bleak expanses of uninhabited moorland were once thriving agricultural communities. However, during the Early Bronze Age the condition of the soil here was completely different; it was sandy and well drained, perfect for farming crops. In fact, it was only towards the end of the 2nd Millennium BC when the climate began to deteriorate rapidly, that increased rainfall caused peat and blanket bog to form on the higher ground, leaving it in its present state. It is thanks to this worsening climate, however, that the ancient monuments in this area are so well preserved.

Unlike on the limestone plateau where over the millennia the pressures of intensive farming have led to the destruction of many ancient monuments, these upland areas have largely remained untouched. Stone circles, barrows and cairns abound.

Each community had its own permanent field systems, houses, crops and livestock, funerary monument and ritual focus – the stone circle. Everything needed was close to hand, rather like the estates of the landed gentry in recent centuries with their manor house, farm, chapel and associated burial ground all defined within the boundaries of one estate.

These Bronze Age monuments are characteristically smaller and more localised, but probably took approximately the same amount of time per person to construct as the larger monuments of the Neolithic. Unlike the earlier sites they are very open, not closed off by large banks and ditches, reflecting the settled family-orientated society of the time. The sheer scale of construction along with the rich grave goods such as pottery Beakers, indicates that society was becoming more organised.

Times of trouble – the advent of the hillfort

This thriving agriculture continued in the British Isles until around 1000BC, when in the Late Bronze Age the major climatic deterioration, referred to above, occurred. This, along with an influx of Celtic peoples from the Continent, led to wide scale changes across the British Isles. The worsening climate placed increased pressure on the land and led to the development of fortified sites known as hillforts, while with the Continental influences the worship focus turned to nature, with water and woodland taking preference over man-made constructions. Consequently, the creation of ritual monuments in the landscape declined.

In addition to the construction of defended hilltop sites, archaeologists have also discovered a large number of 'hoards' where prestigious metal and pottery items were deliberately concealed and never exhumed. By 600BC, a scarcity of copper and tin led to the widespread introduction of iron, the perfect substance for creating strong, powerful weapons. All of these things point to an increasingly hostile society with warfare coming to the forefront.

Archaeological techniques

To discover more about these ancient sites, constructed in a time long before written records existed, we are reliant almost entirely on the science of archaeology. Archaeologists must gather what information they can from the artefacts and structures that survive both above and below the ground, no matter how small or apparently insignificant they may seem.

In general, the climate in the UK is not friendly to archaeology. However, certain types of soil are more conducive to the preservation of certain items. Stone artefacts and structures tend to survive all over the UK, apart from those recycled by man in later millennia, whereas organic materials are much rarer. Bone is sometimes well-preserved in dry alkaline soils like those over chalk, while items like wood, textiles, leaves, animal skin, leather and hair tend to survive only in wet conditions such as peat bogs, where a lack of oxygen impedes the growth of bacteria and thus prevents rotting.

Bones and teeth, both human and animal, are of particular interest. When examined closely, they can tell archaeologists a great deal about how a particular creature lived and died. For example, human bones can show evidence of disease and injury, fatal wounds and other abnormalities as well as revealing the age and sex of an individual. In the case of animals slaughtered for meat, marks left on the bones provide clues to butchery techniques and indicate which were the favourite cuts.

Even the smallest fragments of bone, from sources such as cremations, are useful to scientists and archaeologists. Cremations in the Bronze Age sense were not like cremations of today where the bones are ground to ash after they have been burnt. Certain bones still survive and it is often possible to tell the age, sex and state of health of a person even from the tiniest pieces.

Environmental archaeologists take soil samples and analyse them to locate insects, beetles, snails, small mammal bones, pollen and seeds. By doing so, they are able to establish what the environment was like and how it changed at certain times in prehistory. For example, soil samples can show the transition from natural forest through clearance to cultivation. Snails are particularly useful for a number of reasons. Certain types of snail only live in certain types of habitat, they are not capable of moving over long distances and when they die they leave their shells behind for us to find.

Dating Methods

Archaeologists use a number of techniques in trying to discover the age of things; the most widely used of which is radiocarbon (or C14) dating. All living things, both plant and animal, contain atoms of two types of carbon, ordinary carbon (carbon 12) and small amounts of radioactive carbon (carbon 14). When any organism dies, the radiocarbon begins to decay and over a number of years turns into nitrogen. Thanks to American scientist William Libby, archaeologists know that after 5730 years the carbon 14 is half way to disappearing. Therefore, by measuring the amount of radiocarbon that survives, scientists can work out roughly when something 'died'. This kind of dating cannot produce a specific year, however. The results provide only a range of probable dates covering a period of a number of years and thus are usually followed by + and -, allowing for a margin of error.

Another more precise method of dating is dendrochronology. This method, based on tree rings (oak trees in the UK), is used on sites where wooden material has survived. Each year as a tree grows, it creates a new growth ring; the climate and environmental conditions of the time determine the pattern created. Trees in the same area lay down the same rings. By gradually working backwards using ancient trees that still survive, timbers from old buildings and other wooden items found on archaeological sites, a master database has been created against which any new artefacts can be compared. This method of dating can be particularly precise if the outer wood, known as the sapwood, survives. Sometimes dendrochronologists can even pinpoint the felling of a tree to a specific season within a particular year.

All of the dates listed in this book are quoted as BC (Before Christ) and AD (Anno Domini – after Christ). However, when reading alternative publications, you may come across the non-denominational terms BCE (Before Current Era) and CE (Current Era), which are becoming increasingly popular. Occasionally dates are also expressed as BP (Before Present) with present actually being 1950, the year to which radiocarbon dating is calibrated.

Antiquarians – Archaeological ground breakers

Finally throughout this guide, we often refer to several pioneers who visited and sometimes excavated the prehistoric sites of the Peak District in the past. Many of the stone circles in Derbyshire were mentioned as early as the 18th century by several of these so-called 'antiquarians'.

The Reverend Samuel Pegge, a cleric from Chesterfield (1704-1796) was one of the earliest men to investigate the archaeological features of the Peak. He published several papers in the journal *Archaeologia* between 1785 and 1787 as well as *The Gentleman's Magazine*. His style is typical of the 18th century, with the most notable of his papers entitled 'A disquisition on the lows or barrows in the Peak of Derbyshire, particularly that capital British monument called Arbelows'.

Also active during the 18th century was Major Hayman Rooke, nicknamed 'The Resurrection Major' by the local Derbyshire gentry because of his fascination with burial mounds. He wrote a number of articles for *Archaeologia* between 1782 and 1789. In 1782, he cut two sections across the barrow at Arbor Low, taking an incredible five whole days rather than the usual afternoon, as was customary with antiquarians at the time! Interestingly, the 'Major Oak' at Edwinstow in Sherwood Forest, reputedly the home of Robin Hood, is named after Rooke. In 1789, Pilkington published the impressively entitled *A View of the Present State of Derbyshire*.

By the 19th century, the Victorian period produced the best-known anti-quarians, William Bateman (1787-1835) and his son Thomas (1821-61), also known as 'The Barrow Knight'. William Bateman was a Derbyshire gentleman who teamed up with a solicitor from Sheffield, Samuel Mitchell (1803-1865), in the 1820s. Together they undertook many archaeological investigations including those at Gib Hill near Arbor Low.

Thomas Bateman was born in 1821 at Rowley in Derbyshire and, following in his father's footsteps, had a brief but noteworthy archaeological career. He is famous for his excavations at hundreds of barrows in Derbyshire, Staffordshire and Yorkshire during the 1840s and 1850s. The results of his work were published in two books, *Vestiges of the Antiquities of Derbyshire* (1848) and *Ten Years' Diggings in Celtic and Saxon Grave Hills in the Counties of Derby, Stafford and York* (1861). One of his most famous excavations was carried out at Arbor Low in the 1840s. Bateman also created a private museum of all the material acquired during his digging in his home at Lomberdale Hall.

These early diggers were not lacking in enthusiasm, but they were often lacking in care, sometimes excavating several mounds in one day. In general, the excavations are quite well documented but one cannot help thinking how much more could have been learnt if the advanced technologies of today had been employed instead.

In the late 19th century, the Salts, Micah the father and Micah the son, undertook a number of excavations around Buxton. Micah, the father (1847–1915) was a Macclesfield-born silk weaver, who later set up a tailoring business in Buxton. A self-taught archaeologist, he investigated a dozen cairns around Buxton as well as Five Wells chambered tomb, the results of which were published by Turner in *Ancient remains near Buxton – the archaeological explorations of Micah Salt in 1899*.

In the early 20th century, several documented excavations took place. In 1901 and 1902, the eminent archaeologist H. St George Gray dug at Arbor Low, the results of which were published in *Archaeologia*, while the Bull Ring was excavated by Salt in 1901 and by Alcock in 1949.

Also during the early part of the century, Storrs-Fox, the then Duke of Rutland, and his gamekeeper, E.H. Peat, were active at Froggatt Edge and Barbrook I, the details of which can be found in an unpublished letter held in the Sheffield University collection. Finally several of the sites on Stanton Moor were dug by the Heathcotes, a father and son from Birchover, in the 1930s and 1940s and reported in the *Derbyshire Archaeological Journal* (*DAJ*). Their finds are housed in a private museum in Birchover.

Maps and their uses

To find the prehistoric sites described in this book you will need to refer – in detail – to maps. Luckily for the British monument hunter and the population as a whole, we have the Ordnance Survey.

In our researches, we consulted a number of maps of differing scales and styles. In the early stages of our search we referred to the Ordnance Survey 'Touring Map & Guide 4' of the Peak District. Although our copy was published in 1995 it was at the old Imperial scale of 1:63360 (one inch to one mile). This is a handy map as the whole of the National Park is covered on one side of the map, but it does not contain all the relevant rights of way. In addition, the 1960 equivalent of this map is an interesting read and a lot more attractive than its more recent counterpart.

The 'Outdoor Leisure' series of maps is the ideal map for locating the sites contained within these pages. The two relevant maps are number 24 'The Peak District – White Peak Area' and number one 'The Peak District – Dark Peak Area'. These maps are produced at the more detailed scale of 1:25000 or 2.5 inches to one mile. The one disadvantage to these maps is that they are double sided, which can make them cumbersome to use.

As referred to earlier, additional to the map search for sites, we consulted many paper and electronic references but we soon found that none of the Ordnance Survey maps contained all the locations listed here. You may find that – like ours – your maps soon become embellished with pencilled annotations.

The Ordnance Survey has also produced a series of historical maps covering different eras in British history (the 'Historical Map and Guide' series). This series includes Ancient Britain and Roman Britain (amongst others).

For those wishing to dig deeper into other aspects of the stones there are the solid geology maps produced by the British Geological Survey. A good starting point is the 1:625000 scale map (10 miles to one inch) South Sheet which covers southern Britain up to just north of Scarborough. In addition, the British Geological Survey has also published a series of guides exploring the geology of Britain in plain English.

Finally, the maps contained in this book are by no means a substitute for Ordnance Survey cartography. Good hunting.

Environmental & Archaeological Conservation

All of the monuments discussed in this guide have been in existence for thousands of years. In order to ensure that future generations can enjoy them as we do please remember the following rules:

* If a site is on private land remember to get permission – if you don't you may face court action and upset the landowner enough to deny future visitors access;

* Follow the 'Country Code' – close gates, keep to paths, control your dog and do not drop litter;

* Most of these sites have been fully excavated already and are highly unlikely to contain anything valuable, so do not dig in the ground around them or disturb the stones themselves;

* Do not mark any stones for any reason with anything. Do not move stones, do not light fires inside or outside the circles, and do not place candles on the stones.

In most cases, damage is done unwittingly, but if everyone follows these simple guidelines then access restrictions are less likely to be tightened.

In addition should you encounter any pollution of the watercourses or environmental crimes such as fly-tipping, then please report them to the Environment Agency on 0800 80 70 60.

Era	Year	Approximate construction dates of the monuments covered in this book	Other British monuments in comparison
Early Neolithic	4500BC		
Early Neolithic	4000BC		
Middle Neolithic	3500BC	Chambered cairns and long barrows.	West Kennet long barrow
Middle Neolithic	3000BC	Henges	Castlerigg stone circle
Late Neolithic	2500BC		Ring of Brodgar, Orkney / Trilithons at Stonehenge / Avebury
Early Bronze Age	2000BC	Stone circles / Round barrows and cremation cemeteries	Bluestones at Stonehenge / Boscawen-ûn stone circle, Cornwall
Middle Bronze Age	1500BC		Mên an Tol, Cornwall / Uffington White Horse
Late Bronze Age	1000BC		
Iron Age	500BC	Hillforts	Maiden Castle hillfort, Dorset

Henges

Henges are unique to the British Isles. There are at least three hundred scattered throughout Britain and Ireland, mainly located in areas that were quite highly populated in prehistory. They range in size from as little as 9m in diameter to an incredible 450m in diameter. Only thirteen known sites, referred to as 'circle-henges', have or had settings of stone within them although excavations at many others have revealed that a large proportion did contain circular features of timber.

Circle-henges are thus relatively rare and the Peak District is fortunate in having two examples so close together, Arbor Low on Middleton Common between Buxton and Ashbourne and the Bull Ring in Dove Holes to the north.

In general, these so-called circle-henges are located down the central spine of Britain from the Ring of Brodgar and the Stones of Stenness on Orkney to the Stripple Stones 1000km to the south on Bodmin Moor in Cornwall. Other examples include the Broomend of Crichie, Balfarg and Cairnpapple in Scotland, the Devil's Quoits, Avebury and Stonehenge all in Wiltshire, and Castelruddery and Grange in Ireland.

Mention of the word 'henge' usually conjures up thoughts of Britain's most famous ancient monument, Stonehenge. This is a unique and complex site with huge trilithons and circle of Bluestones, but it does not actually fit the archetypal description of a henge monument. A henge is defined by archaeologists as 'a roughly circular earthen banked enclosure, usually with an internal ditch and one or more entrances, which may or may not have inner settings of timber or stone'. At Stonehenge, the ditch is actually external to the bank and thus atypical.

Within the general description of henge monuments, academics have often made a further division: Class I henges with one entrance, dating from the late 4th to late 3rd millennium BC, and Class II henges with more than one entrance, dating from around the middle of the 3rd to the 2nd millennium BC. Of the Class II henges, the most common type are those with a pair openings opposite one another. Both Arbor Low and the Bull Ring fall into this category.

As to their use, henges were essentially neutral places where our Neolithic ancestors came together to trade items such as highly prized stone axes or special places where tribal groups could meet for ritual purposes. It has been suggested that between them the two Derbyshire henges would have been the tribal focus for most, if not all, of the Peak's inhabitants at the time.

John Barnatt believes that Arbor Low and the Bull Ring, placed either side of the natural boundary of the Wye gorge, would have been adequate meeting places for the Neolithic tribes of the north and south respectively. There may originally also have been many smaller ritual monuments on the limestone plateau but these have disappeared over the millennia as the pressures of agriculture in these fertile areas led to increased demands on the land. It is unlikely, however, that any other large-scale henge monuments were destroyed by such intensive farming.

The Neolithic landscape essentially saw the first man-made architecture on a grand scale. For the people living in small farming communities in primitive wooden houses, it must have been an awe-inspiring experience to visit a site on the scale of Arbor Low or the Bull Ring. Evidence suggests that many henge monuments were deliberately constructed in such a way as to further enhance the impact they had on visitors. For example, due to the topography at Arbor Low, the profile of the high bank is only visible when approached from the north and the northern entrance is much wider than its counterpart, suggesting this direction was intentionally chosen to be the main way in.

In addition, views of the interior were often restricted from most areas outside a henge, apart from at the causewayed entrances where onlookers would see all the way through. Some of the larger monuments had what have been called 'blocking devices' or coves in the interior. The rituals carried out in these areas would not have been visible to any but the elite who were privileged enough to be allowed inside.

As to what rites did take place at henges, we can only guess. Some archaeologists have suggested that they may have been used as astronomical observatories, but with such a large bank the people within the monument would not have been able to see out to distant horizons, apart from at the entrances. At Arbor Low, for example, the north-west entrance is roughly aligned with the setting of the midwinter full moon, but the view from the cove looks towards the south-south-west and is blocked by the huge earthworks within 30 metres. Thus any astronomical alignments, apart from those directly above, would not be seen from here.

Another explanation is that they were connected with the rituals of death. As Aubrey Burl points out 'In the New Stone Age, death and the dead obsessed the living'. In addition to the obvious funerary sites such as the chambered tombs and barrows, this statement is also true of henges and the later Bronze Age stone circles. Many have human remains buried somewhere within them. Both whole skeletons and fragments of cremated bone are found in stone-lined graves, known as cists, in decorated pottery vessels or urns, either under barrows and cairns or at the base of standing stones. These may just be votive offerings, however, rather than graves in the sense we know them today.

Whatever their associations it cannot be disputed that henges were some kind of communal ritual focus for our Neolithic ancestors. The sheer scale of the monuments proves that there must have been an organised society, with people working together to create their 'sacred landscapes'. Recent research has shown just how much effort was involved in the construction of such sites. It has been estimated that it would have taken 10,000 working man-hours to erect a long barrow and a million man-hours to create a henge (Souden, 1997). All this would have been accomplished using primitive tools such as ox shoulder-blade shovels, antler picks and rakes, bone wedges and flint and stone chisels, axes and adzes. The sheer amount of red deer antlers used in such construction, as well as in the mining of stone and flint for the tools, seems to suggest that Neolithic man must have been breeding and managing his own animals (Mercer, 1998).

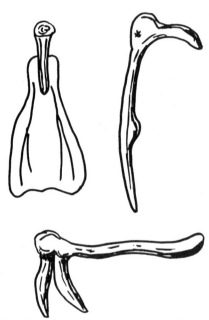

Undoubtedly a large communal effort would have been required to first prepare the land, construct the bank and ditch, quarry and transport the stones, then dress and erect them. Even with today's technological advances, it is still a skilled process to shape and erect stones of such large proportions. When considering that the only technology available to our Stone Age ancestors was wood, rope and human/animal power, (they didn't even have the wheel) it is a miracle that they were ever erected at all, as recent attempts by modern scientists have often proved!

To return to the Peak District, the two Derbyshire circle-henges are characteristically very alike.

Ox shoulder-blade shovel; antler pick; antler rake

Construction of both monuments probably began in the Late Neolithic period (circa 3000BC to 2000BC), both are located on the limestone plateau, both continued to be used into the Bronze Age, both are very similar in size, both have two entrances and both originally had stone settings within them. The only main differences being that the Bull Ring no longer has any stones and is placed in a low lying area, whereas Arbor Low is situated higher up on a plateau.

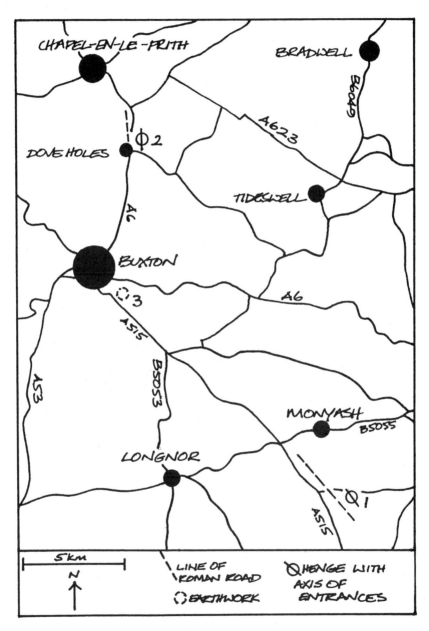

Henge Monuments of the Peak District: Site 1: *Arbor Low circle-henge; Arbor Low II earthworks.* **Site 2:** *The Bull Ring circle-henge.* **Site 3:** *Staden earthworks*

Site 1

Arbor Low henge, stone circle and barrows, Parsley Hay, Middleton Common, Derbyshire

Map reference: SK160636

Access

Arbor Low is well signposted from the main Buxton to Ashbourne road (A515). A small car park is provided just inside the entrance to Upper Oldhams Farm, situated off the road known locally as Back Lane (parking is also available on this lane). The farmer leases the land and manages the site for English Heritage. A small fee is charged for entrance (at the time of writing it is 50p for adults and 25p for children). Follow the path through the farmyard to a stone stile, following the path up to the left for Arbor Low. A walk of about 10 minutes will take you up the hill to the splendour of the stones. After prolonged spells of wet weather the path does become very muddy so you may need a pair of wellies!

Details

Often referred to as 'The Stonehenge of the North', Arbor Low is described on the small fading English Heritage noticeboard as 'One of the most important prehistoric monuments in Britain'. Located on a plateau 375m (1230ft) above sea level, it contains a number of interesting features. The name Arbor Low is said to be a corruption of *Eorthburgh Hlaw* possibly of Saxon derivation, meaning 'Earthwork mound'. It is the only stone circle in Derbyshire constructed from limestone, although it is possible that if the Bull Ring's stone settings had remained, they would also have been made from local limestone.

As with its famous Wiltshire counterpart, the circle-henge at Arbor Low was almost certainly constructed in a number of phases during the 3rd millennium BC, evolving to reflect the changes in society. The long barrow of Gib Hill close by (GR: SK158634) was probably the original worship focus on the site before the oval bank and ditch of the henge, with its two entrances to the north-west and south-south-east, were established in the Late Neolithic period. The stones were added later and were almost certainly in place by 2000BC.

Use of the site continued into the Bronze Age when the most prominent part of the outer bank was reconstructed to allow for the erection of a large round barrow. At this time, the balance of power in society was shifting from a communal focus to a dominant elite. The barrow was, therefore,

The recumbent circle-henge of Arbor Low, often known as the 'Stonehenge of the north'

probably created as a bold political statement by a high status individual. This burial mound, clearly visible today on the south-eastern bank of the henge, remained 'an antiquarian problem' for many years, and was excavated on no less than four occasions in antiquity. In 1770, the then occupier of the farm investigated without success, as did Major Rooke in 1782 and William Bateman and Samuel Mitchell in 1824. Upon the fourth attempt in 1845, however, Thomas Bateman struck lucky.

To quote the barrow knight himself 'The 23rd of May, 1845, is an important day in the annals of barrow-digging in Derbyshire, as on that day was made the discovery, so long a desideratum, of the original interment in the large tumulus, which forms one end of the southern entrance to the temple of Arbor Lowe, and which had been unsuccessfully attempted on previous occasions by three parties of antiquities' (Bateman, 1848).

On that historic day, Thomas cut across the barrow from the south side discovering a shoulder blade and the antler of a large red deer in the process, before locating a small six-sided limestone cist. Inside this he found a quantity of calcinated human bones, a kidney shaped flint instrument, a pin made from the leg-bone of a small deer and a piece of iron pyrites along with two decorated pottery urns.

Thomas Bateman had previously also excavated another barrow, located a few metres beyond the round barrow on the henge bank, on the 8th October in 1844. Measuring roughly 10m by 11m, this barrow had obviously been robbed at an earlier date and contained nothing more than an empty grave and 'a piece of very much oxydised iron' which resembled the socket of a spear-head. It is likely that this burial was much later, perhaps even Romano-British (dating to the first half of the first millennium AD).

The sacred site of Arbor Low now consists of a ruined circle (actually egg-shaped) of around fifty large locally quarried limestone blocks with seven smaller blocks in the centre forming an open box, known as a cove, close to which the human skeletal remains were discovered.

Described by Aubrey Burl as 'reclining like pallid sunbathers', all but one of the stones are now recumbent with only one to the west-south-west remaining partially upright. Some of the fallen, broken stones do appear to fit together, indicating there were probably between forty-one and forty-three standing stones originally. They are of varying shapes and sizes ranging from about 1.6m to 2.1m in height, with the exception of the monoliths at the entrances which are between 2.6m and 2.9m tall. The stump of one stone, perhaps the remains of a portal stone, can be found in the southern entrance while a large pit in the northern entrance indicates this may also have contained a stone.

The oval earthen bank is approximately 90m by 85m externally in diameter and 2m high, with the inner platform of 52m by 40m. The surrounding ditch is circa 2m deep and between 7m and 12m wide. The bank and ditch are broken by two causewayed entrances that are not exactly opposite, one 9m wide to the north-west and one 6m wide to the south-south-east.

The positioning of henge entrances is a topic that has attracted the attention of various academics in recent years. It has been suggested that having two causewayed entrances, Class II henges were ritual monuments that were either designed to be passed through, with one opening an entrance and the other an exit, or had one entrance for onlookers and one for those conducting ceremonies. The former appears to be more plausible as the axes of henges are often placed along the same lines as well-used ancient routes. They are rarely positioned in the direction of other monuments. At Arbor Low, for example, neither of the entrances points towards Gib Hill, while on Orkney, the Ring of Brodgar is aligned along the isthmus, the route of the modern road, rather than pointing to other archaeological features in the area.

Such alignments are interesting because Arbor Low itself actually lies within 400m of the Roman road known as 'The Street' which ran from Buxton to a settlement at Carsington Pastures close to Brassington. In his article, Loveday notes a statistical correlation between the alignment of nearby Roman roads and the axis of Class II henge entrances. Clearly, the

Roman roads are far more recent than the henge monuments, but the Romans would have used pre-existing tracks. Does this alignment indicate that these ancient trackways were in some way connected to the ritual of the henges or is it pure coincidence?

Although the henge is believed to have been a communal monument, it is interesting to note that even when they were fully upright, the stones would not have been visible from outside of the bank. Even looking in through the entrances, the huge stones of the central cove, which are much taller at 3.9m and 4.25m, were positioned in such a way (opening to the south-south-west) that the people outside would not have been able to see what was happening in this inner sanctum. The centre of the site was obviously a place reserved only for the initiated conducting their sacred rites.

Coves are relatively rare in the British Isles and often only found at large complex monuments. Believed to have been imitations of the earlier Neolithic burial chambers, they are unroofed structures, usually composed of two side slabs and a backstone. Other known examples include those at Stanton Drew in Somerset, Avebury in Wiltshire and at the Standing Stones of Stenness on the Isle of Orkney.

Between 1901 and 1902, H. St George Gray (an eminent archaeologist who also worked at the world famous site of Avebury between 1908 and

One of the huge cove stones from the sacred area in the middle of the circle

1922), undertook archaeological investigations in the main henge and circle at Arbor Low. Under the auspices of the Anthropological Section of the British Association, operations took place from the 8th to the 23rd August, 1901 and for ten days in May and June, 1902. A number of local miners from Monyash were employed to assist with the digging.

Gray began his search in the area of the ditch. Close to the southern entrance he found thirteen ox teeth and pieces of red deer antler, which he deduced may have been the remains of a pick used to excavate the ditch originally. Close to the other entrance, he discovered six flakes of black flint and a sheep's tooth. Elsewhere a number of stone implements were found including various flint and chert arrowheads and scrapers.

The most interesting discovery occurred, however, when Gray turned his attention to the area in the interior of the stone circle. Close to one of the central stones, to the south-east of the centre of the circle, the skeleton of an adult human male was discovered. It lay on its back with the face turned slightly to the north-east and was surrounded on three sides by large blocks of stone. Interestingly the top of the head was pointing to the south-south-east, the exact direction of the second smaller entrance.

Over the years, several other important artefacts have been discovered in the area of the henge, but sadly their positions were never recorded, so we cannot ascertain how they are connected. These finds include a bronze spearhead, a flint dagger, a stone macehead, some polished flint knives and a stone adze.

Finally, there has been much debate as to why the stones at Arbor Low are no longer standing or indeed if they ever stood at all. Some believe it is because they had insufficient support at their base, while others suggest people who literally feared what they 'stood' for deliberately and maliciously felled them. Aubrey Burl proposes that the stones were blown over by the winds from the north, because they lie inward at the north and outwards at the south.

As mentioned above, the standing stones are composed of limestone, a rock that is mildly water-soluble. This would undoubtedly have contributed to the collapse of the stones that may have been weakened at the base after centuries of standing in wet soil. The destructive power of water on limestone is further evident on the surfaces of the fallen monoliths where potholes and cavities were created by torrents flowing over the bedrock many millennia before the rocks were hewn.

There are others who even believe that the stones never stood at all, based on the findings of Gray. During his excavations in the early 20th century, he tested the area around the base of one of the stones and failed to find a stone hole. He only examined this one stone, however, which is naturally flat and wide at the base, and so may have stood on its own anyway.

Many of the stones are also badly broken which implies that they have fallen with some force rather than being recumbent from construction. The most telling piece of evidence however, is the fact that upon close inspection one of the stones, to the west-south-west, is still partially standing while the vertical stumps of others are evident elsewhere in the ground.

In addition, some antiquarians report speaking to people who actually remembered seeing stones in an upright position. In 1783, Dr Pegge reports that "the stones formerly stood on end, two and two together, which is very particular". Glover in his *History of the County of Derby* (1829) writes "Mr J. Pilkington was informed that a very old man living in Middleton, remembered when a boy to have seen them standing obliquely upon one end". Even Gray himself was told by one of his excavators, described as 'an old man', that he had "seen fives stones standing in his boyhood and had sheltered under them!" Gray nevertheless then adds, "On inquiry, however, I ascertained that the man had a reputation for gross exaggeration".

One stone can be seen further down the hill next to one of the dry-stone walls of the farm. Several other stones may also have been removed by local farmers and workmen for building material, such as gateposts and lintels.

Gib Hill

Gib Hill Barrows, near Arbor Low, Middleton Common, Derbyshire

Map reference: SK158634

Access

Gib Hill has been included in this section of the book, simply because it is located approximately 300m to the south-west of Arbor Low circle-henge. It can be reached either by walking along the path from the south-west entrance of the henge or by following the signposted path up the hill from the farmyard.

Details

As Arbor Low has been described as 'The Stonehenge of the North', so Gib Hill has been called 'A miniature Silbury Hill'. It appears at first glance to be a fine example of a Bronze Age round barrow, however, archaeological evidence reveals that it is actually two barrows with a Bronze Age round barrow superimposed on top of an earlier Neolithic long barrow. This long barrow was probably the original ritual focus in the area several hundred years before the henge monument of Arbor Low was created.

An earthwork avenue running south-south-west from the bank of the henge leads most of the way across the field to the barrow, suggesting that the two were perhaps once linked. The grassy mound itself is sometimes known as the 'serpent' and may have been constructed at the same time as bank of Arbor Low, although some believe it could be nothing more than a field boundary.

As with the barrow on the henge monument, Gib Hill was also excavated on several occasions. In the early 19th century, the then tenant, a Mr Normanshaw is reputed to have found a human skull while, in 1812, the landowner, a Mr Thornhill, discovered some human bones and Roman coins.

In 1824, William Bateman and Samuel Mitchell investigated the site and excavated a mound in the middle of the barrow containing some charcoal, cremated human bone, a flint arrowhead and a fragment of 'basaltic celt'. Other flints and a small iron brooch were found closer to the surface. The site was unsurprisingly also excavated later by Thomas Bateman in 1848. In the typical style of the early archaeologists, he removed the main limestone burial cist that contained a food vessel and cremation. It had reputedly fallen through the roof of his tunnel while he was digging, and

The possible earthwork avenue leading from the bank of the henge at Arbor Low towards Gib Hill to the south-west in the background

was relocated into his own garden at Lomberdale Hall! Thankfully it was returned in 1938 and is still visible today resembling a capstone on the top of the mound.

Gib Hill is reputedly named after a gibbet which once stood there in the 18th century, however, recent research at other sites has shown that the origin of this name may lie further back in the distant past. As exposed in Channel 4's 'Secrets of the Dead' (July 2000), an Anglo-Saxon man was beheaded at Stonehenge in the late 7th century AD. Further investigations brought to light the fact that double-posted gallows (very similar to the trilithons themselves) had been erected close to the site. In fact, the name Stonehenge itself actually drives from the Old English *stanhengen*, which means 'hanging stones'.

The programme revealed that by the Dark Ages, ancient sites had become associated with superstition and fear; new kingdoms were being established and the rulers of these needed to prove their power. Thus significant wrongdoers and outcasts were executed and buried at places such as Stonehenge which were outside the normal limits of society, a tradition which continued for hundreds of years. Even in 18th century Derbyshire, murderers and suicides were treated thus. A reference in Youlgreave Parish Church records an incident in 1779 when men were paid money for carrying corpses to the Bronze Age cemetery of Stanton Moor 'To ale and bread and cheese to ye men for carrying corpses to Stanton Moor'. Other British barrows named after gallows include Gallow Howe in Yorkshire, Gallow Hill near Salthouse in Norfolk, Coombe Gibbet long barrow in Berkshire and Gibbet Knoll in Wiltshire.

A second possible henge site, known as Arbor Low II (GR: SK157633) lies to the north-west of Gib Hill. Consisting of a curved ditch, some archaeologists believe it may be an unfinished henge, but others consider it is probably nothing more than a ditch created as a result of stone quarrying in the area.

Comments

In 1848, Thomas Bateman wrote of Arbor Low 'were it not for a few stone fences, which intervene in the foreground, the solitude of the place and the boundless view of an uncultivated country are such as almost carry the observer back through a multitude of centuries, and make him believe that he sees the same view and the same state of things as existed in the days of the architects of this once holy fane'.

J.D. Sainter subsequently commented in 1878 'It commands an extensive prospect and the feeling of visiting the place upon a fine summer's day, when there is no sound to disturb the solitude except for the singing of the lark and now and then the cry of the plover (which here abound), are most pleasing; still this is accompanied by a certain amount of reverential awe and amazement, especially on a first visit, when contemplating this hoary ruin along with its eventful history'.

These sentiments are still largely true today. Apart from the farm buildings at the bottom of the hill, the views are still mostly unspoilt by modern construction. The atmosphere at the henge seems to change depending on the time you visit. Sometimes it can be frustrating when you are distracted by the chatter of fellow visitors, while on other days you can find yourself there alone and really begin to experience the ambience of the place.

There can be no doubt that the Arbor Low site is of major significance both on a local and regional level as well as in a nation-wide context. It is unique in the Peak District in that it combines nearly all of the major archaeological features described in this book in one place and its long and colourful history bears testament to this. It was a ritual focus for both the living and the dead, a place where whole tribes could assemble to venerate the remains of those long past. The sheer scale of the monument shows just what a commitment the local people must have put into building it.

Other Sites close by:

Site 10 – Nine Stone Close stone circle, **Site 24** – Bee Low round cairn, **Site 33** – Castle Ring hillfort, **Site 34** – Cratcliff Rocks hillfort, **Site 36** – Cranes Fort.

References and Further Reading

W. Anthony "Haunted Derbyshire and the Peak District", Breedon Books Publishing Company, Derby (1997)

J. Barnatt "The Stone Circles of the Peak", Turnstone Books, London (1978)

J. Barnatt "The Henges, Stone Circles and Ringcairns of the Peak District", Department of Archaeology and Prehistory, University of Sheffield (1990)

J. Barnatt and K. Smith "Peak District, Landscapes through Time", English Heritage & B.T. Batsford Ltd, London (1997)

J. Barnatt, R. Manley and G. Short "Arbor Low a guide to the monuments", Peak National Park Authority (1996)

A. Burl "A Guide to the Stone Circles of Britain, Ireland & Brittany", Yale University Press (1995)

A. Burl "Prehistoric Henges", Shire Publications, Princes Risborough (1997)

A. Burl and M. Milligan "Circles of Stone The Prehistoric Rings of Britain and Ireland", Harville Press, London (1999)

J. Cope "The Modern Antiquarian", Thorsons (1998)

H. St.George Gray "Arbor Low Stone Circle; excavations in 1901 and 1902", *Derbyshire Archaeological Journal*, volume 26 (1904)

L.V. Grinsell "The Ancient Burial Mounds of England", Methuen & Co, London (1953)

J.C. Heathcote "Bronze Age Cist from Gib Hill", *DAJ*, volume 61 (1940)

R. Loveday "Double Entrance Henges – Routes to the Past?", In *Prehistoric Ritual and Religion*, edited by Alex Gibson and Derek Simpson, Sutton Publishing, Stroud (1998)

J.D. Sainter "Scientific Rambles Round Macclesfield", Silk Press reprint, Macclesfield (1999)

P. Wroe "Roman Roads in the Peak District", *DAJ*, volume 102 (1982)

Site 2

Bull Ring henge and barrow, Dove Holes, Derbyshire

Map reference: SK078785

Access

The second of the region's circle-henges is located on open land just off the main Buxton to Chapel-en-le-Frith road (A6) in a little village called Dove Holes. It can be found immediately behind St Paul's Church next to the Dove Holes Community Centre and Sports Fields. Although it is not on a public footpath, there are no known access restrictions.

The best way to find the henge is to park on the minor road opposite the railway station. Walk back towards the village and you will come to a drive leading to the recreation ground (signposted 'Welcome to Dove Holes Community Association'). Follow the track round to the right past the car park and the sports changing rooms and you will see the henge (or what's left of it) in front of you.

Details

Located in a low-lying area of the limestone plateau on the main route to the Cheshire Plain, the Bull Ring is similar in both size and design to Arbor Low. However, it is believed to have had all of its stones removed in the 18th century, perhaps taken for building material or used during work on the nearby road. Again the henge was constructed in the Late Neolithic (circa 3000BC to 2000BC) and was perhaps a neutral area where people came together to trade. It also has entrances that mirror the alignment of a Roman road running close by, from Buxton to the Fort at Melandra near Glossop.

It is unclear how the monument came to be called the Bull Ring, but it has been suggested that it may perhaps once have been used for bull baiting or was at one time an enclosure for keeping bulls in. Alternatively, being an impressive earthwork 'ring', it may just have been naturally prefixed with the word 'bull' to form the name common elsewhere.

The Bull Ring is typical of the condition of many British henges. Unlike most stone circles that have mystical appeal, henge monuments have often been forgotten and neglected. The once impressive earthwork banks have been eroded or ploughed almost flat and the ditches have silted up. Some only survive as crop marks, visible from the air at certain times of the year. Compared to some, the Bull Ring is still noticeably recognisable as an ancient monument, but it is nevertheless still sadly in a rather dilapidated state considering it did once have a stone circle. Only the bank, internal quarry ditches and two entrances, placed exactly north and south, now remain.

Today the henge has an external diameter of approximately 90m and an internal diameter (to the edge of the ditch) of about 46m by 50m. It is not easy to calculate the original dimensions of this monument as millennia of abuse have altered its appearance. As with Gib Hill at Arbor Low, there is a large mound to the south-west of the Bull Ring. No known excavations have been carried out on this, however. It even seems to have escaped the attentions of Thomas Bateman!

There are several documented accounts of the henge in recent centuries. When Pilkington visited the Bull Ring in 1789, he noted that one stone remained. At this time, local residents had constructed a dry-stone wall from entrance to entrance and the whole area was under cultivation. By the 19th century, the north-east section of the ditch had been severely damaged by quarrying. A skeleton was discovered during work, but nothing was ever recorded.

Excavations were undertaken by Salt and others in 1901 and later by Alcock in 1949. Salt discovered a few finds in the ditch, including shards of pottery and some flints, while the 1949 excavations revealed an ox molar, some fragments of bone, seven flint scrapers and knives and several more pieces of pottery.

The circle-henge of the Bull Ring at Dove Holes. Today, only the earthworks survive.

Even in the 20th century destruction of the site continued. In 1905, W.J. Andrew F.S.A. was so concerned about the fate of the Bull Ring that he wrote a short article in the *Derbyshire Archaeological Journal* asking for it to be preserved. He writes 'The object of this short notice is to direct attention to the fact that this remarkable monument stands in imminent peril of total destruction from the approach of the great lime works, which are now within a comparatively few yards of its bound. Can it be saved?'.

Ten years later, Edward Tristram F.S.A., also in an article about the Bull Ring in the *Derbyshire Archaeological Journal,* reports 'A few yards to the south-east is an immense excavation made by the local lime works, which a few years ago, threatened the total demolition of the Bull Ring. Happily, this catastrophe was averted for the time being owing to the exertions of some Buxton archaeologists'.

More recently, a spotlight (now gone) was erected in the centre of the monument along with a cable trench that cut across archaeological features. In addition, bonfires were held for many years on the site, a car park and changing rooms have been erected over the features at the northern entrance and most of the top soil has been stripped off.

Comments

The Bull Ring is unique in the Peak District in that it is the only one of the surviving megalithic monuments currently located within a modern community. Today, surrounded by playing fields, football pitches, a church and houses, without stone settings and greatly eroded, it is hard to imagine how majestic it must once have looked. The henge is still very much close to the centre of village life, but its use is now recreational rather than ceremonial. Considering its importance, it is surprising to find that there is no acknowledgement on the site as to its status as an ancient monument.

One other point of interest is that there is a church located within metres of the henge. As with many other ancient sites around the country, over the millennia the worship focus has shifted from pagan to Christian. The most famous example of this can be found at Knowlton in Dorset, where a derelict 12th Century Norman church stands in the centre of a large Neolithic henge. At Stanton Drew in Somerset, St Mary's Church lies 300 metres to the south-west of the great stone circle, close to the cove, while on Glastonbury Tor, the tower of St Michael's stands proudly at the centre of a prehistoric hillfort. At Toller Porcorum church in Dorset the 1,400-year-old wall collapsed earlier this century, revealing two prehistoric standing stones that had been embedded deep within the structure.

It is often believed that round churchyards were once ancient places of worship with earlier sites being used for later religious purposes. It is also highly likely that many of the carved crosses and inscribed stones, particularly common in Cornwall and Wales, are recycled Bronze Age standing stones.

Other Sites Close by:

Site 3 – Staden earthworks, **Site 30** – Castle Naze hillfort, Buxton Museum.

References and Further Reading

W.J. Andrew "The Bull Ring: a stone circle at Dove Holes", *DAJ*, volume 27 (1905)

J. Barnatt "The Stone Circles of the Peak", Turnstone Books, London (1978)

J. Barnatt "The Henges, Stone Circles and Ringcairns of the Peak District", Department of Archaeology and Prehistory, University of Sheffield (1990)

J. Barnatt with assistance from A. Myers "Excavations at the Bull Ring Henge, Dove Holes, Derbyshire, 1984-85", *DAJ*, volume 108 (1988)

E. Tristram "The stone circle known as the 'Bull Ring', at Dove Holes, and the adjoining mound", *DAJ*, volume 37 (1915)

W. Turner "The Bull Ring Doveholes", The Leek Times, August 23rd, 1902

P. Wroe "Roman Roads in the Peak District", *DAJ*, volume 102 (1982) near Buxton, Derbyshire

Site 3

Staden earthworks

Map reference: SK069721

Access

A third possible henge is located a mile outside Buxton, just off the main Buxton to Ashbourne road (A515) on the edge of a little industrial estate. Travelling along the A515 out of Buxton, take the first road on the left; sign posted 'Ashbourne road Industrial Estate'.

The road crosses a railway line almost immediately by a small bridge. Go left at once after this bridge, to Staden Business Park. The vague traces of an earthwork circle can be seen in a field, to the rear of the industrial units owned by Northern Electrical Factors and Buxton Tool Hire Ltd. (shown on the OS map as the third field along before the industrial estate was built).

Details

Unlike the Bull Ring and Arbor Low, Staden is dubiously referred to as a henge. It consists merely of a circular bank, approximately 58m by 53m in diameter, with a rectangular bank adjoining, rising no more than 0.3m above the surrounding field, with an internal ditch and maybe one or two entrances. Recent research has been carried out on another later feature close by which may bring into question the definition and date of these earthworks.

In 1926, a Romano-British settlement (enclosure) was discovered 180 metres to the north of the Staden earthworks on a piece of ground known as Limespiece, belonging to Buxton Corporation. Archaeologists unearthed numerous animal bones and teeth, fragments of Roman pottery, chert and flint chippings, half a polished axe and several pieces of ornamental bronze from the 1st or 2nd century AD. The site was also investigated again in 1983 when in addition to further pottery dating from around the 2nd century AD, archaeologists also discovered more evidence of early prehistoric activity in the area when shards of Neolithic Grooved ware and flints were found within the enclosure. As to how or if these discoveries relate to the Staden earthworks, we will not know until someone carries out an excavation on them.

Other Sites Close by:

Site 2 – Bull Ring henge and barrow, **Site 19** – Five Wells chambered cairn, **Site 30** – Castle Naze hillfort, Buxton Museum.

References and Further Reading

J. Barnatt "The Stone Circles of the Peak", Turnstone Books, London (1978)

J. Barnatt "The Henges, Stone Circles and Ringcairns of the Peak District", Department of Archaeology and Prehistory, University of Sheffield (1990)

G.A. Makepeace with contributions from P. Beswick and M. Bishop "The Romano-British Settlement at Staden near Buxton: The 1983 Excavations (with Archival Material concerning the 1926 Excavations)", *DAJ*, volume 107 (1987)

Stone Circles

There are over one thousand prehistoric stone circles in Britain and Ireland, of which twenty-six examples are located in the region of the Peak District. Some, such as Arbor Low and Nine Stone Close, have been well-known for years. Others such as Eyam Moor II and III and Doll Tor were mentioned by antiquarians but then lost for generations, while Gibbet Moor North and Ash Cabin Flat were only discovered as recently as the 1980s, following the burning of the surrounding moorland vegetation.

Located at the southern end of the Pennines, the prehistoric stones of the Peak District appear to form a lonesome assemblage in the middle of England, with the nearest groups of any significant number located some distance away in North Wales and the Lake District. All of the stone circles in the Peak District were constructed within a few hundred years either side of 2000BC in the Early Bronze Age, about the time the Bluestones were erected at Stonehenge. However, unlike the UK's most famous ancient monument, all of the Peak rings were constructed from local stone, readily available in the immediate locality.

In comparison to the huge stone circles of southern England and northern Scotland, the Derbyshire stone circles are characteristically small both in height and diameter. Most consist of a ring of upright stones set into a bank, (embanked stone circles) although there are a number of variations. Some have no bank at all (free-standing circles) while others have a bank but no standing stones (ringcairns), and although they are all referred to as 'circles' many are actually slightly elliptical in shape.

They were undoubtedly constructed as some kind of special place, a focal point and sacred centre for the community, but we can only guess at their actual purpose. Archaeology tells us who built them and when, but it does not reveal the secrets of the mysterious ceremonies held within.

Perhaps they were connected with astronomy – many of the megaliths in the British Isles show some sort of alignment with the heavens, particularly the midsummer and midwinter sun and moon rises. The annual rotation of the sun is significant in cultures the world over with particular emphasis placed on the four main divisions of the year – the summer solstice (around June 21st) and winter solstice (around December 21st) along with the vernal equinox (around March 21st) and autumnal equinox (around September 21st).

At Stonehenge on the morning of the summer solstice, the sun rises over the Heel Stone. At Newgrange in Ireland, only on the day of the winter solstice do the rays from the sunrise shine through a special opening above the

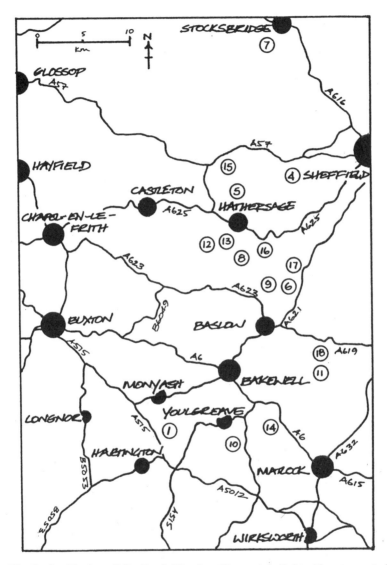

The Stone Circles of the Peak District: Site 4: *Ash Cabin Flat stone circle.*
Site 5: *Bamford Moor South stone circle.* **Site 6:** *The Barbrook Group.*
Site 7: *Ewden Beck stone circle.* **Site 8:** *The Eyam Moor Group.* **Site 9:** *Froggatt
Edge stone circle.* **Site 10:** *Nine Stone Close stone circle.* **Site 11:** *Park Gate Stone
circle.* **Site 12:** *Smelting Hill Stone Circle.* **Site 13:** *Offerton Moor stone circle.*
Site 14: *The Stanton Moor Group (see also Stanton Moor map).* **Site 15:** *Seven
Stones of Hordron stone circle.* **Site 16:** *Lawrence Field, possible stone circle.*
Site 17: *Brown Edge stone circle.* **Site 18:** *Gibbet Moor North stone circle.*

entrance and illuminate the 24 metre, stone-lined passage of the chamber deep within the mound. At Nine Stone Close in Derbyshire the major southern moon, around midsummer, sets between the pillars of Robin Hood's Stride overlooking the circle, while at the Rollrights in Oxfordshire an entrance to the south-east is almost directly in line with the rising of this same southern moon.

Alternatively, stone circles could be the ancient equivalent to our churches, sacred places where rituals associated with birthrights, marriage, death and seasonal festivals were performed. Many have also been connected to fertility. You only have to look at the shape of certain stones to understand why.

Why circles? As previously mentioned, none of them are true circles, most are slightly longer in one direction making them more oval in shape. This indicates that they were perhaps laid out by eye and made to look round rather than being geometrically perfect. Nowadays living in our square houses with right angled corners and straight walls it seems unnatural for things to be circular, but ancient man obviously had his reasons. Perhaps it is because a circle is the easiest shape to create well, or maybe it is because in a circle there is no hierarchy – everyone is equal in status, just like the Knights of King Arthur's Round Table. This would fit in well with the then newly found vision of communal spirit rather than rule.

On the other hand, perhaps we should look to nature for the answer. In the natural world there are few straight lines, but many circles. The glowing orb of the rising and setting sun, the glimmering golden circle of the ripe full moon, the ripples on a lake, the rings on a tree, the centre of a flower, even the irises of the eyes, the windows of the soul. Nature is full of all things circular, so why shouldn't our ancestors have recreated what was natural to them?

These days with light pollution, roads, cities, cars and modern science it is almost impossible to imagine just what it would have been like living in an outdoor world with nothing but the elements, not really understanding why everything happens as it does. As a farmer, man would have been more susceptible to the forces of nature than ever before. The passing of the seasons, the patterns of the weather, an abundant crop and healthy livestock were all essential parts of farming life.

For us the stones will always hold a magical appeal, most importantly because no matter how much we try, we will never really know why ancient man built them or what they were used for.

Finally, many of the stone circles described in this chapter are located on bleak expanses of moorland, often overgrown by bracken, heather, bilberry and peat. For this reason, they are often not particularly photogenic, but this should not deter anyone from making a personal visit, enabling the size, shape and atmosphere of the monuments to be truly appreciated.

Site 4

Ash Cabin Flat stone circle, Derbyshire

Map reference: SK269863

Ash Cabin Flat is a circle we finally discovered on our third attempt. It is definitely a site to be visited in the winter or spring, as it is hard enough to find on the boulder strewn moorland without having to contend with waist high bracken covering less than knee high stones.

Access

Ash Cabin Flat is located south of the A57 Manchester to Sheffield road. Park in the car park at the end of Redmires Road, just before the Redmires reservoirs, at GR: SK269859. Immediately after the notice board, a footpath leads off to the left, climbing up through the trees.

After five to ten metres, when you reach the dry-stone wall, the main footpath swings round to the right, whilst a rough track leads to the area of the stone circle. Ash Cabin Flat, the stone circle, is not actually marked on the map, but is located within 100m of the dry-stone wall in an area now covered in a dense mass of heather and bracken.

The best way to locate it is to follow the line of the dry-stone wall until it starts to become ruinous and slopes gradually down hill. The circle is immediately due east in the direction of Wyming Brook farm, which is visible in the distance.

Details

This site of Ash Cabin Flat contains the smallest circle in Derbyshire and stands on a shelf of land above Wyming Brook. It was only discovered as recently as 1981 when the surrounding moorland vegetation was burnt away.

Only two of the stones are now standing, set into the edge of an embankment, but there are a couple of others close by which may once have formed part of the circle. The bank is very small, approximately 9m by 7.5m in diameter and between 1m and 2m wide with no apparent features inside and no entrances. The centre is flat. A few small cairns have also been located to the south of the circle following the burning of the heather.

Comments

Ash Cabin Flat is really nothing more than a slight bump in an area of exposed moorland and very difficult to locate. The most prominent stone to the south is diamond-shaped and this is the most recognisable feature when searching for the circle.

Although it is small and damaged, it is one of those sites where one can get away from the distractions of modern life (apart from the roar of the motorbikes in the distance on the nearby A57 on a warm summer's day).

The diamond-shaped southern stone of Ash Cabin Flat, one of the circle's only distinguishing features

Other Sites close by:

Site 5 – Bamford Moor South stone circle, **Site 15** – Seven Stones of Hordron stone circle, **Site 16** – Lawrence Field possible stone circle, **Site 29** – Carl Wark hillfort.

References and Further Reading

J. Barnatt "The Henges, Stone Circles and Ringcairns of the Peak District", Department of Archaeology and Prehistory, University of Sheffield (1990)

J. Barnatt "Taming the Land: Peak District Farming and Ritual in the Bronze Age", *Derbyshire Archaeological Journal*, volume 119 (1999)

Site 5

Bamford Moor South stone circle, Bamford Moor, Derbyshire

Map reference: SK221845

Access

One of the ways to find this site is to turn off the A625 Castleton to Hathersage road at Hillfoot (GR: SK219818) onto an unnamed minor road. After approximately 600m turn left into Coggers Lane and follow this up the hill to a T-junction, where you should bear round to the left. Continue along for about 1.5 km at SK226841, then follow the road sharp left; this will take you up Bole Hill.

After about a kilometre you will descend into the Upper Hurst Brook valley. When the road levels out on the other side of the valley, you will see a grassy lay-by adjacent to a footpath (GR: SK215839). Obviously there are several ways to get there, but do beware, some of the minor roads in the area are 'not suitable for motor vehicles'.

Navigation is very difficult on this bleak, featureless moor, however do not be put off because there is a well-preserved circle to be found for those who persevere. Following the map, you should take the footpath due north for 900m until you come to a dry-stone wall (with associated ditch). Follow it in a south-easterly direction, keeping along the line of this wall until it ends. The circle lies 100m or so to the east-north-east.

Unfortunately, on the ground this is easier said than done. Our mistake was to go up through the quarry (marked on the map) rather than following the path round to the east. The main problem is that this footpath is only very narrow in places and does become easily hidden by the growing heather.

Details

Once you find the circle, your efforts will be well rewarded. Bamford Moor South is a well-preserved embanked stone circle, offering views through 180 degrees, with the rocky spine of Stanage Edge and High Neb to the north-east and the wooded area of Dennis Knoll to the south-east. (You can actually see the Dennis Knoll car park from the circle, although there is no footpath leading to it.)

One of the smallest sites in the Peak District, the circle is a little over-grown by heather, but all the stones are still visible set in the inner edge of a bank. They form a ring approximately 8m by 7m in diameter. We counted eight large stones on site, but only six forming part of the circle. One stone,

located to the west, is noticeably taller than the others, about 0.75m in height, while the others are closer to 0.5m.

The circle is built on a slight slope and terraced into the hillside thus making the embankment, which is approximately 11m in diameter, more prominent to the south and west.

Comments

Bamford Moor South is a smaller circle than most, but perhaps because of this it is also more complete. The surrounding moorland is not particularly pictur-esque, although the views from the circle are quite impressive.

The tallest stone of Bamford Moor South, orientated to the west, where the bank is more prominent

The rock climbers in the vicinity and the cars in the nearby car park are an ever-present reminder of the modern world. And yet – if you lie back and close your eyes, apart from the occasional faint voices of the people high up on Stanage Edge carried on the breeze, you can easily imagine that you are slipping back into the past.

Other Sites close by:

Site 4 – Ash Cabin Flat stone circle, **Site 8** – The Eyam Moor Group (three stone circles and barrow), **Site 12** – Smelting Hill stone circle, **Site 13** – Offerton Moor stone circle, **Site 15** – Seven Stones of Hordron stone circle, **Site 16** – Lawrence Field possible stone circle, **Site 29** – Carl Wark hillfort.

References and Further Reading

J. Barnatt "The Stone Circles of the Peak", Turnstone Books, London (1978)

J. Barnatt "The Henges, Stone Circles and Ringcairns of the Peak District", Department of Archaeology and Prehistory, University of Sheffield (1990)

Site 6

The Barbrook Group

The collection of prehistoric monuments known as 'The Barbrook Group' is situated on the large area of gritstone moorland between Sheffield and Bakewell, the Eastern Moors Estate, in the area of Big Moor and Ramsley Moor.

The whole area is littered with numerous cairns and ancient stones, all of which are located within a protected wildlife and heritage Sanctuary Area. Access to parts of the Eastern Moors Estate is restricted by the Peak District National Park Authority (the owner) in order to protect the wildlife, ecology and widely distributed archaeological interests within the Estate. The Peak District National Park Authority does however grant specific access for scientific or educational purposes. Anyone wishing to visit the Barbrook sites for such reasons should apply in writing to the Peak District National Park Authority in Bakewell.

In order to ensure that these important sites remain preserved for millennia to come, please respect the restrictions in place.

The large cairn located to the north-east of Barbrook I, restored in the 1960s following disturbance by antiquarians

Barbrook I stone circle, Big Moor, Derbyshire

Map reference: SK279756

Details

Barbrook I is one of the best preserved stone circles in the Peak District. A typical example of an embanked Derbyshire stone circle, it is similar in many ways to the Nine Ladies on Stanton Moor, although unlike Stanton Moor, Big Moor is, for the reasons explained overleaf, a very deserted area.

Commanding a spectacular vista over a mass of purple heather in the summertime, the circle of twelve stones sits in a hollow on a shelf of raised ground on the exposed gritstone moorlands. On a clear day, the views to the south-west extend to the limestone ridges and plateau some ten miles distant, while in other directions the circle overlooks the vast expanse of Big Moor and Ramsley Moor.

A worn rubble bank, 19m by 17m in diameter, surrounds the circle of stones, 12.5m by 14.5m. The bank is built on a gradual slope and is therefore more prominent to the south-west where the land gradually falls away. A gap in the ring exists to the north-east, which may originally have contained one more standing stone.

The well-preserved stone-circle of Barbrook I looking towards the limestone plateau in the distance

A close up of one of the Barbrook stones showing signs of weathering, where millennia of raindrops have worn deep channels into the rock

The stones are all of differing shapes and sizes, although only one situated to the south-west is taller than one metre. Some show signs of weathering on the top, as at many other sites, particularly the two closest to the track.

The remains of two trenches dug earlier this century by the Duke of Rutland's Gamekeeper, E.H. Peat, are still visible inside the circle. During this excavation, only a few flints, now in the Buxton Museum, were discovered. These trenches along with the ditch were also re-excavated in 1987, in order to recover further environmental evidence.

Comments

Barbrook I is one of the most enigmatic and best-preserved sites in the Peak District. It has an incredible aura, helping us to appreciate why our ancestors chose to build such a monument there. Standing in the middle of the circle the 21st century is soon forgotten, as this is one of those rare places where past and present are almost one.

Barbrook II stone circle, Big Moor, Derbyshire

Map reference: SK278758

Details

Barbrook II stone circle is not marked on any of the maps but is located 600m to the north-north-west of Barbrook I. Between the two circles is an interesting cairn or barrow situated immediately above Barbrook I (to the north-east). This cairn is a notable site in itself. The cairn as it now stands was excavated in the 1960s having been previously disturbed, like many in this area, by antiquarians. During excavation, fragments of cremated bones and pieces of pottery from a collared urn were discovered in the centre,

The dry-stone wall at Barbrook II, into which nine standing stones are set

along with an urn covering the cremated bones of a child. Four stones, now in the store at Sheffield Museum, were also found to be decorated with prehistoric cup and ringmarks.

The Barbrook II stone circle itself is of a similar size to Barbrook I, consisting of an irregular set of nine (originally ten) stones set into a low dry-stone wall, 14.5m by 13.5m in diameter, 3.5m wide and 0.5m high, with one entrance to the north-east.

A small cairn is located in the interior. Only one of the standing stones, to the west-south-west, is taller than the surrounding wall, but there does not appear to be any special reason why this should be so.

Barbrook II was first documented in 1850, in an unpublished letter to Thomas Bateman from Samuel Mitchell. The latter had excavated the site but revealed nothing of significance.

G.D. Lewis carried out further excavations between 1962 and 1970, when the whole of the interior, a cairn located in the entrance and the main bank were investigated. A number of cupmarked stones were discovered both in the bank and elsewhere on site (see the *Rock Art* section for further details). During the 1969 season, four human cremations were also discovered within the enclosure, two in simple pits, one below the cairn and another in a small stone cist. Radiocarbon analysis from the cremation under the central cairn gave a date of circa 2192BC to 1430BC, placing it firmly in the Bronze Age.

Around the midsummer solstice in 1988 and 1989, the circle was crimi-

The small cairn inside the circle at Barbrook II, under which a cremation was discovered during excavations in 1969

nally altered by 'persons unknown'. The stones were placed upright in completely the wrong positions, the wall was made higher with stones robbed from elsewhere and the cist was even turned into a fireplace! The monument has now been fully restored to look as it might have done circa 2000BC, following partial re-excavation in October and November 1989 by the then Peak Park Joint Planning Board in consultation with English Heritage.

Following this restoration, eight of the ten stones were replaced in their original stone holes. The ninth could not be located but was substituted with a similar stone. The excavations also revealed that the four standing stones to the north and west were in deep holes, whereas those in the other half were shallower. They were also found to be placed very unevenly, so much so that John Barnatt, Senior Survey Archaeologist for the Peak District National Park Authority, comments 'This is the only extensively excavated site in Britain where spacing can be shown to be this irregular'. The archaeological finds can be seen in the Sheffield Museum.

Comments

Barbrook II is most unusual, quite unlike any other stone circle we have ever seen. In fact, it is more reminiscent of a dry-stone wall or sheep enclosure rather than a megalithic monument.

Although located in close proximity to Barbrook I, the first circle is not visible from here, as it is located in a slight hollow. The whole area must

*One of the stones in the wall of Barbrook II, now replaced in its original stone
hole following restoration in 1989*

have been of great significance during the Bronze Age and it is especially
interesting to find two such enigmatic circles so close together. Similar
groupings are found in the Peak District in the regions of Stanton Moor and
Eyam Moor.

Barbrook III stone circle, Big Moor, Derbyshire
(also known as Owler Bar)

Map reference: SK283773

Details

Located on the top of a flat ridge below Flask Edge, to the north-east of
Barbrook stream and reservoir, Barbrook III is another illustrative example
of a typical Derbyshire stone circle. It is very rare in that given the large
number of stones involved, it appears to be almost complete. The views
from the site are extensive, but the circle itself is very difficult to make out,
as most of the stones are almost completely overgrown by the moorland
grass and partially covered in peat.

Due to the fact that the circle is buried to some extent, it is hard to tell
exactly how many stones there are – we counted nineteen, but there are

some other outliers which could form part of the main circle, possibly twenty-one in total. The stones, mostly leaning or collapsed, stand in a bank approximately 26m by 23.5m in diameter, making it one of the largest circles in the Peak District. The bank is broken by three gaps, with one to the east-north-east most noticeable which may have been the original entrance.

Comments

Of the three stone circles on the moor, Barbrook III is the most difficult to distinguish. The views are nevertheless very picturesque and because the area is so quiet and deserted, it is easy to appreciate the appeal of the place and imagine how important it must once have been.

This was one of the first sites we visited and only now, looking back with hindsight, do we realise how rare it is to find a large circle where virtually all the stones have remained in situ. Most of them are fallen, partially buried and overgrown, but nevertheless, remain in almost exactly the same position in which our Bronze Age ancestors placed them thousands of years ago. At so many other sites in the region and in the country as a whole, ancient stones have suffered at the hands of modern people, carried off as building material for walls, gates and door posts or recycled into aggregate for road building.

There are two other sites of interest on this moor, but due to their isolated location and poor condition, they are only really of interest to the keen enthusiast. We have not actually visited them ourselves, but brief details are mentioned below.

Barbrook IV stone circle/ringcairn, Ramsley Moor, Derbyshire (also known as Ramsley Moor)

Map reference: SK289756

Situated on the edge of Ramsley Moor, east of Barbrook I, on the edge of the Foxlane Plantation, Barbrook IV is marked on the map as a cairn. It has sometimes been referred to as a stone circle, but is more likely to be a ringcairn. All that remains is a rubble bank circa 23m by 21m externally in diameter.

Common in northern Britain, ringcairns are composed of a circular bank of rubble and small stones, enclosing an area in which burials were placed. They are very similar in character to the embanked stone circles apart from the obvious difference of a lack of standing stones. Occasionally a few burials occur in their bank as well as the interior.

Barbrook V stone circle/ringcairn, Big Moor, Derbyshire (also known as Big Moor)

Map reference: SK269751

Part of an extensive cairnfield, Barbrook V is located to the west of Barbrook I, on the other side of the Bar Brook stream. It is also more likely to be a ringcairn, rather than the remains of a stone circle. It has been badly damaged by a packhorse track which cut through the centre in the Medieval period. Only half of the bank to the south-east remains.

Other Sites close by:

Site 8 – The Eyam Moor Group (three stone circles and barrow), **Site 9** – Froggatt Edge stone circle, **Site 16** – Lawrence Field possible stone circle, **Site 17** – Brown Edge stone circle, **Site 18** – Gibbet Moor North stone circle, **Site 26** – Gardom's Edge (Neolithic enclosure, barrow and prehistoric rock art), **Site 29** – Carl Wark hillfort.

References and Further Reading

J. Barnatt with contributions from F.M. Chambers "Recent Research at Peak District stone circles including Restoration work at Barbrook II and Hordron Edge, and new fieldwork elsewhere", *DAJ*, volume 116 (1996)

J. Barnatt "The Stone Circles of the Peak", Turnstone Books, London (1978)

J. Barnatt "The Henges, Stone Circles and Ringcairns of the Peak District", Department of Archaeology and Prehistory, University of Sheffield (1990)

J. Barnatt and K. Smith "Peak District, Landscapes through Time", English Heritage & B.T. Batsford Ltd, London (1997)

J..Barnatt and P. Reeder "Prehistoric Rock Art in the Peak District", *DAJ*, volume 102 (1982)

A. Burl "A Guide to the stone circles of Britain, Ireland & Brittany", Yale University Press (1995)

J. Cope "The Modern Antiquarian", Thorsons (1998)

Site 7

Ewden Beck stone circle, Derbyshire
(also known as Broomhead I)

Map reference: SK238966

Access

To locate the circle of Ewden Beck, you will need to take the road across Bradfield Moors, known locally as Mortimer Lane, which joins the A616 (T) in the north to the A57 Glossop to Sheffield road in the south. Park in the lay-by opposite Broomhead Hall (GR: SK242962) on this road.

A footpath marked by a sign reading 'Footpath to stone circle' leads off to the north-west. After approximately 500m, it divides into three paths, just after passing over the beck (dry in July). The path straight ahead is a private track, marked 'no right of way', while the main footpath, marked by another sign, forks at 45 and 90 degree angles to the right. The path at 90 degrees is the one you need. The stone circle is located approximately 100m down and is marked by a tall wooden post.

Details

Ewden Beck is the most northerly of all the known sites in the Peak District to the north-west of Sheffield and west of Stocksbridge and marked on the map as 'enclosure'. The circle is named after the nearby stream of Ewden Beck and is located on a flat shelf just above the steep valley, in an area surrounded by a bank and ditch of unknown date. As far as the view is concerned, there is very little to see in any direction.

It was believed that an extensive prehistoric cairnfield lay to the south and west of the stone circle. This appeared on Ordnance Survey maps and has even been scheduled as an ancient feature. However, on a recent inspection John Barnatt of the Peak National Park Authority failed to find a single cairn that was a convincing example. He believes that the features are nothing more than 'natural knolls, fortuitous natural stone concentrations and more recent features associated with surface quarrying'.

Ewden Beck consists of eight or possibly nine stones (five of which are still standing) in a ring 16m by 14.5m set into the inner edge of an earthen bank. The stones vary in height between about 0.75m and 0.35m, hence the difficulty of recognising not only the stones amongst the vegetation, but also the definition of the ring.

Walking along the path, the first of the stones you will come to is located within 6m of the wooden post, at the northern entrance of the circle. It is about 0.5m tall and is leaning to the left. Two metres to the right of this is another stone, rather square and boulder-like in appearance and also approximately 0.5m in height. If you walk between these two, after about 12m, you will come to the tallest stone at the southern entrance, with its long axis running almost exactly north/south. Immediately behind this is another large stone, now recumbent.

The largest stone at the southern entrance of Ewden Beck; probably one of the most distinguishing features of the circle

The bank, now barely visible, is approximately 20m in diameter and between 2m and 3m wide into which a single stone is placed to the south-east. To the east, it is particularly high where the ground behind drops away. Other stones lie close by and may once have formed part of the ring. Two entrances, to the north-north-west and south-south-east, both edged with stones are located in the bank, and there are two cairns within the circle. If the stones were evenly spaced there may have been as many as fourteen or fifteen originally, with four stones at the entrances.

Comments

This site is quite complex and very similar to the circle on Froggatt Edge. Originally it would have had two pairs of stones flanking the entrances, which are placed exactly opposite (north-north-east and south-south-west in the case of Froggatt and north-north-west and south-south-east in the case of Ewden Beck) in addition to stones set into both the inner and outer edges of the bank.

Due to the undergrowth and the apparent randomness of the stones, this is a pretty unimpressive circle. The ring is not clearly defined and is therefore difficult to visualise. Even in the depths of winter, the vegetation obscures many of the features.

Other Sites close by:

Ewden Beck is a lonesome stone circle with nothing close by. However, being on the outskirts of Sheffield, it could be combined with a trip to the Sheffield Museum in Weston Park.

References and Further Reading

J. Barnatt "The Stone Circles of the Peak", Turnstone Books, London (1978)

J. Barnatt "The Henges, Stone Circles and Ringcairns of the Peak District", Department of Archaeology and Prehistory, University of Sheffield (1990)

J. Barnatt "Taming the Land: Peak District Farming and Ritual in the Bronze Age", *DAJ*, volume 119 (1999)

Site 8

The Eyam Moor Group

Eyam Moor is located above the village of Eyam. The latter was famous in the 17th century as being the only place outside London where a major outbreak of the Great Plague (1665 to 1666) occurred, during which the lives of 260 inhabitants were claimed.

The wild moorland has a number of ancient features, hidden amongst its vegetation, including three stone circles several barrows and a cairnfield. Described by Thomas Bateman in 1848, the area around Eyam Moor appears to have been rich in prehistoric archaeology:

'Numerous urns have been found at various times around Eyam; a richly-ornamented urn containing ashes was found in making an occupation road at the time of the inclosure; more recently, two men working near the Bole Hill, Eyam, discovered an urn surrounded with stones, which they broke in hope of a sudden accession of treasure, but were disappointed on finding it filled with ashes; amongst which were two Roman coins in small brass, one of which was Maximianus Hercules'.

To reach this group, we took the B6001 south from Hathersage (a turning off the main A625 Chapel-en-le-Frith to Sheffield road). There are several ways to find the moor; one is to turn right off the B6001 about 1.5km south of Hathersage (this turning is not signposted) and follow the minor road through Hazelford to Leam.

The footpath onto the moor can be found opposite Leam Hall (not Leam Farm). An alternative route (if, like us, you miss the first turning) is to continue along the B6001 until you reach Grindleford. Take a right turn opposite the 'Sir William Hill' public house and climb up a steep hill; after about a kilometre you will come to the footpath and Leam Hall.

All the stone circles on the moor can be reached from the same point by climbing the stile opposite the entrance to Leam Hall (GR: SK231794) and following the well-worn path steadily uphill onto the moor. Your first point of reference is the point where a dry-stone wall (marked on the OS map) crosses the path. For reasons of ease, we have listed the sites in the order in which you will come to them, rather than in numerical order.

Eyam Moor II stone circle, Derbyshire

Map reference: SK231789

Access

Following the path up from Leam Hall, you will reach Eyam Moor II first. The circle is very overgrown with heather and bilberry and is located approximately 40m from the wall and path intersection, immediately on the edge of the path to the east (left). Look for the circular mound of vegetation.

Details

Mentioned on several occasions by antiquarians, Eyam Moor II stone circle was only rediscovered in 1983, which is rather surprising considering its close proximity to the well-used footpath.

This embanked stone circle is now somewhat ruined and submerged. One of the smallest sites of Derbyshire, it is approximately 8m by 7.5m in diameter with only four low stones, ranging in height between 0.15m and 0.3m, set into the bank. After searching around in the bilberry for several minutes, we eventually managed to locate two of these stones.

The circle is constructed on a gradual slope with the bank and ditch more prominent to the west and east. There is a break to the north-north-west, which may originally have been an entrance and a disturbed cairn in the centre.

Although lost for many years the existence of this site, along with Eyam Moor III, was known previously and was perhaps mentioned by Thomas Bateman in 1852. He notes 'a tumulus within a circle of nine stones, six only of which remain upright, the diameter of this circle is 14 yards, near to this is a mound enclosed by a circle of seven stones, the inner diameter of which is eleven yards'. These descriptions fit well with Eyam Moor II and III stone circles.

Comments

As with many other sites, to give yourself a chance of seeing anything at all, you should definitely avoid going in the height of summer when the vegetation is abundant. Also, being located so close to a footpath be prepared for perplexing looks from fellow walkers when scrabbling about in the undergrowth.

Eyam Moor III stone circle, Derbyshire

Map reference: SK232788

Access

Eyam Moor III was also only relocated in 1983 and is to be found about 200m down hill to the south-east of Eyam Moor II. The easiest way to find it is to look for the corner where the dry-stone wall boundaries meet – the circle is less than 100m from the eastern edge of this structure.

Details

Eyam Moor III is quite unusual in that it is one of only five surviving free-standing stone circles in the Peak District. The others are the Seven Stones of Hordron, Doll Tor, Gibbet Moor North and Nine Stone Close.

The circle itself is approximately 13m by 12.5m in diameter. We counted six stones in total, two of which are recumbent. The stones are of the typical Derbyshire height (up to 0.75m) although the collapsed ones would almost certainly have been taller, perhaps over a metre when standing.

If this is the second site referred to by Thomas Bateman in 1852, then fortunately it would appear that only one stone has gone missing in the meantime. Assuming even spacing, there may have been eight originally. Perhaps the builders of the nearby dry-stone walls saw an easy opportunity to make use of the stone.

In the middle, there is a dumbbell-shaped cairn structure, in a north-south alignment, with a trench cut through the centre. The inside has been excavated out to reveal patches of the cairn's internal stone structure.

Comments

Eyam Moor III stone circle is also very overgrown with vegetation, although unlike its neighbour to the north-west, the stones here are clearly visible and cannot be missed.

As on Stanton Moor and Big Moor, the close proximity of several stone circles indicates that these areas were highly important during the Bronze Age. One wonders why our ancestors felt the need to build two circles so close together. Perhaps individual families were keen to stamp their authority on the land and by constructing a circle within view of their neighbour's they were making a bold territorial statement.

Wet Withens stone circle, Derbyshire
(also known as Eyam Moor I)

Map reference: SK225790

Access

Wet Withens is located on a flat area of land towards the northern end of Eyam Moor and is difficult to locate especially if the heather is in season, although it is marked on the map. Starting at the first reference point where the dry-stone wall meets the path, walk due west for about 600m, which could be quite difficult unless you go in the winter or spring when the vegetation has died back.

You should see Eyam Moor barrow first – a large pile of stones accompanied by a sign. Technically Eyam Moor barrow falls into the category of a cairn, being composed of a mound of stones rather than earth, but often in the Peak District this type of stone burial monument is described as a barrow. Other well-preserved examples include the barrow to the north of Barbrook I stone circle and those on Gardom's Edge.

The barrow itself, now oval in shape may originally have been circular, as it was known as 'Round Hillock' in the 18th century when it was attacked by stone robbers in 1759, who reputedly found various objects dating to the middle Bronze Age.

The recognisable form of Eyam Moor Barrow, located immediately to the north of Wet Withens stone circle

On reaching the barrow, the circle is about 10m from the back end of it to the south.

Details

Wet Withens, sometimes known as Wet Withers (Old English for 'the wet land where willows grew'), is the largest embanked stone circle in Derbyshire. Located on a slight slope, just above the 335m contour, to the west of an extensive cairnfield, the ten or eleven millstone grit uprights are placed at the inner edge of a continuous bank. The bank is approximately 31m by 29.5m internally in diameter, between 2m and 3m wide and 1m high and, most unusually, it has no entrances. In addition, a small cairn lies to the south-east of the centre.

Seven of the stones are still standing, but most of them are leaning and all are less than a metre in height, barely projecting above the level of the bank. The tallest stone, to the north-east, is about 0.70m tall and shaped like a chair (as our daughter Megan was quick to discover!). It also has three interesting circular indentations on the back that may be cupmarks, but could just as easily be natural. Nine of the stones, including the tallest, are carved with the initials 'FU' and one with an illegible date.

The antiquarian Thomas Bateman writing in 1848 mentions that when a Mr Wood visited the site earlier in the 18th century he noted 'sixteen oblong masses of sandstone standing in an upright position, forming a circle about thirty yards in diameter'. However, when Bateman finally vis-

Nine of the stones at Wet Withens bear signs of modern graffiti, carved with the initials FU, perhaps by some local landowner

ited the circle himself in 1852, only thirteen stones remained and by 1860, when Wilson went, there were only ten on site.

Wood also mentions that a further large stone, then removed, had stood in the centre some years previously. Also in the vicinity were at least twelve cairns composed of a large heap of stones, under which urns had been found.

Comments

Of all the stone circles visited, Wet Withens has to be one of the most atmospheric. High on the moor away from footpaths and people, once the circle has been found, its remote yet impressive setting makes a considerable impact with an overriding sensation of the loneliness of the site. Since it is quite a way off the beaten track, you are less likely to be disturbed by others.

The panoramic views are only interrupted by Eyam Moor barrow immediately to the north and the gently rising slope of Eyam Moor to the south. Beyond the barrow, the eye wanders towards the valley below and on to Hathersage partially hidden by High Low. To the east, the wooded slopes of the Derwent Valley give way to Bole Hill and Lawrence Field nearly 3km away.

Other Sites close by:

Site 5 – Bamford Moor South stone circle, **Site 6** – The Barbrook Group (3 stone circles, a barrow, 2 ringcairns and numerous small cairns), **Site 9** – Froggatt Edge stone circle, **Site 12** – Smelting Hill stone circle, **Site 13** – Offerton Moor stone circle, **Site 16** – Lawrence Field possible stone circle, **Site 17** – Brown Edge stone circle, **Site 29** – Carl Wark hillfort, **Site 31** – Burr Tor hillfort.

References and Further Reading

J. Barnatt with contributions from F.M. Chambers "Recent Research at Peak District stone circles including Restoration work at Barbrook II and Hordron Edge, and new fieldwork elsewhere", *DAJ*, volume 116 (1996)

J. Barnatt "The Henges, Stone Circles and Ringcairns of the Peak District", Department of Archaeology and Prehistory, University of Sheffield (1990)

J. Barnatt "The Stone Circles of the Peak", Turnstone Books, London (1978)

J. Barnatt and K. Smith "Peak District, Landscapes through Time", English Heritage & B.T. Batsford Ltd, London (1997)

T. Bateman "Vestiges of the Antiquities of Derbyshire", London (1848)

A. Burl "A Guide to the stone circles of Britain, Ireland & Brittany", Yale University Press (1995)

Site 9

Froggatt Edge stone circle, Derbyshire (also known as Stoke Flat)

Map reference: SK249768

Access

There are several ways of finding Froggatt Edge stone circle, but for easy access and a gentle walk it is perhaps best to start at the north of the Edge. Park in the lay-by (GR: SK265776) on the B6054 road to Froggatt or in the National Trust Haywood car park across the road. (If you park in the car park, there is a path at the bottom end which takes you back to the road – this involves crossing a small stream on stepping stones).

Walking back down the B6054, approximately 200m on the left, you will see a marked footpath accessed via a white gate. Follow the footpath south through the trees and after a further 600m you will cross a stream and come to another gate. Froggatt Edge circle is about 150m through the gate, to the left (east) of the path.

The circle can also be reached from the footpath leading from the Chequers Inn public house (GR: SK247760), south of Froggatt. However, this means quite a steep uphill climb through the trees.

Details

Froggatt Edge stone circle is set on a flat shelf, overlooking the picturesque Derwent Valley to the west and Eyam Moor to the north-west. The circle can become very overgrown with bracken, so again it is best to visit when the vegetation has died back.

Often referred to as Stoke Flat, the site is complex, though now sadly quite ruined. Very similar in design to Ewden Beck, it consists of an embanked stone circle with two entrances exactly opposite, to the north-north-west and south-south-east. Traces of dry-stone walling in the northern entrance suggest that it may have been deliberately blocked at some time in prehistory.

The bank is approximately 2m wide, 11.5m internally and 15.5m externally in diameter. Both entrances are lined with a set of parallel stones, with four remaining in the southern entrance and three in the northern one. Elsewhere four smaller stones are set at the inner edge of the bank. It is clear that there are quite a few missing and may have been as many as sixteen originally.

The majority of the stones are of typical Derbyshire height, about 0.5m

tall, while the largest stone, flanking one of the entrances, is over 1m in height. As with several other Peak District circles, this tallest stone stands to the south-west and has deep weathering grooves on the top and down the sides.

Froggatt Edge was again partially excavated in the early 20th century by the Duke of Rutland and his gamekeeper, E.H. Peat, (the same pair who dug the trench across Barbrook I), but nothing was found.

Comments

The largest stone of Froggatt Edge standing prominently to the south-west

The circle stands at the north-western end of a large cairnfield and a large cairn is located immediately to the south. Although rather ruined, it is still an interesting place. Particularly of note is the tallest stone, which really stands out and bears witness to many millennia of exposure to the elements. Sadly, the site is located close to a very well-used footpath, so if it is peace and quiet you want, Froggatt is not the place to go at the weekend.

Other Sites close by:

Site 6 – The Barbrook Group (3 stone circles, a barrow, 2 ringcairns and numerous small cairns), **Site 12** – Smelting Hill stone circle, **Site 13** – Offerton Moor stone circle, **Site 16** – Lawrence Field possible

Modern offerings show the site of Froggatt Edge is still revered today

stone circle, **Site 17** – Brown Edge stone circle, **Site 26** – Gardom's Edge (Neolithic enclosure, barrow and prehistoric rock art).

References and Further Reading

J. Barnatt "The Stone Circles of the Peak", Turnstone Books, London (1978)

J. Barnatt "The Henges, Stone Circles and Ringcairns of the Peak District", Department of Archaeology and Prehistory, University of Sheffield (1990)

A. Burl "A Guide to the stone circles of Britain, Ireland & Brittany", Yale University Press (1995)

Site 10

Nine Stone Close stone circle, Harthill Moor, Derbyshire (also known as The Grey Ladies)

Map reference: SK225626

Access

The stone circle is situated within view of the rocky outcrop known as Robin Hood's Stride, which is a good landmark when looking for the site. Nine Stone Close can be found by following the narrow road from Alport to Elton (known locally as Cliff Lane). Approximately half way along the lane, the stones become visible in a field to the east of the road and are reached via a signposted footpath through the fields. Please note, however, that the stones are a short distance from the footpath on private land. Parking for a small number of cars is available on the road in a lay-by (GR: SK224627).

Details

Nine Stone Close is one of the few free-standing circles in the Peak District, now consisting of only four stones, composed of local gritstone and located in the eastern half of a circle which was probably originally between 13.5m and 12m in diameter. There is a great deal of evidence to suggest that when the circle was created it was considerably larger, perhaps even comprised of as many as nine stones as the name implies.

Thomas Bateman describes the site in 1848 as 'a small druidical cirque, about thirteen yards in diameter, now consisting of seven rude stones of various dimensions. . . the circular area inclosed within the boundary of the stones is somewhat elevated, so as to appear as a low tumulus, but it has never been explored'. Bateman also notes that two other stones of similar dimensions stood 'eighty yards to the south'.

Nine Stone Close differs from the other surviving circles of the region in that the stones are much larger, about 2m high and above, although the stones at Arbor Low would have been taller, if they were still standing. Old illustrations show that the absent stones were perhaps somewhat smaller than the four now remaining. One of the missing stones seems to verify this conjecture for it can still be seen, used as a gatepost in a nearby dry-stone wall to the south of the field.

The site was partially restored in 1939, following the collapse of one of the stones in 1936, which had been leaning badly for several years. It was also decided to re-erect another stone that had lain flat since prehistoric times. With equipment 'kindly loaned' by Messrs. Ackroyds of Birchover, the two fallen stones were re-erected and cemented in place.

One of the missing stones, now used as a gatepost in the wall to the south of the standing stones

Circular indentations on the back of one of the stones, caused by the weather rather than being man-made

As with many other sites in the Peak District, the stones show signs of rilling – i.e. simple weathering grooves running down from a hollowed out area on the top. These look almost like basins in which to catch the rain, from where it is channelled, down the edges of the stones. It is interesting to note that the stone which had lain recumbent since ancient times has weathering grooves on the side, rather than the top, suggesting it must have fallen over hundreds, if not thousands, of years ago.

Many other monuments in the area have similar weathering patterns, which are particularly noticeable on the tallest stones. Some of the best examples include Barbrook I, Froggatt Edge and the Seven Stones of Hordron.

Comments

There are several conflicting local traditions about the Nine Stones. Some state that on moonlit nights the Grey Ladies come to life and can be seen dancing; others believe that the 'nine' may actually be a derivation of 'noon' because traditionally the stones are mostly associated with dancing at midday.

It seems more likely that the position of the ring is connected with the moon, explained by the outcrop of Robin Hood's Stride (GR: SK223623) which loiters to the south of the Grey Ladies. During the midsummer moonrise, the moon passes between the Stride's pillars. This impressive neighbour must surely have been a source of inspiration to the stone builders and would have provided a spectacular setting for rituals and ceremonies at the circle. A prehistoric rock carving found on the Stride in the 1970s, indicates that it was perhaps considered a special place by our ancestors (see the *Rock Art* section for further details).

Described by Aubrey Burl as 'the head and pricked up ears of a wrinkled hippopotamus', it is believed that the Stride almost certainly takes its name, not from Robin Hood, the famous green-clad outlaw of Sherwood Forest, but from the ancient 'Green Man' of the woods, the fertility god of pagan legend. It is also known locally as Mock Beggars Hall, due to the pinnacles that are said to resemble chimneys creating the appearance of a house in silhouette.

As at many other sites a number of unusual sightings have been reported in and around the area of the Nine Stones. On one occasion a strangle blue light was seen to come out of the woods and hover above the stone circle, while at numerous other times claims have been made of sightings of fairies!

Also of interest, just behind the main outcrop, is a cave known as the Hermit's Cave. Here at Cratcliff Hermitage, believed to have been used over several centuries, a crucifix has been carved into the rock showing the area was still of spiritual significance, even thousands of years after the stone circle was built.

Other Sites close by:

Site 1 – Arbor Low (circle-henge, barrows and Gib Hill), **Site 14** – The Stanton Moor Group (5 stone circles, Andle Stone, Cork Stone and numerous smaller cairns), **Site 20** – Minning Low chambered round cairn, **Site 21** – Green Low chambered cairn, **Site 24** – Bee Low round cairn, **Site 27** – Rowtor Rocks prehistoric rock art, **Site 33** – Castle Ring hillfort, **Site 34** – Cratcliff Rocks hillfort, **Site 35** – Ball Cross hillfort, **Site 36** – Cranes Fort.

References and Further Reading

W. Anthony "Haunted Derbyshire and the Peak District", Breedon Books Publishing Company, Derby (1997)

J. Barnatt "The Stone Circles of the Peak", Turnstone Books, London (1978)

J. Barnatt "The Henges, Stone Circles and Ringcairns of the Peak District", Department of Archaeology and Prehistory, University of Sheffield (1990)

J. Barnatt and K. Smith "Peak District, Landscapes through Time", English Heritage & B.T. Batsford Ltd, London (1997)

J. Barnatt and P. Reeder "Prehistoric Rock Art in the Peak District", *DAJ*, volume 102 (1982)

A. Burl "A Guide to the stone circles of Britain, Ireland & Brittany", Yale University Press (1995)

J. Cope "The Modern Antiquarian", Thorsons (1998)

J.P. Heathcote "The Nine Stones, Harthill Moor", *DAJ*, volume 60 (1939)

Site 11

Park Gate stone circle, near Beeley, Derbyshire

Map reference: SK281685

Access

From the village of Beeley, which is located approximately 2km to the
south of Derbyshire's famous Chatsworth House, follow the windy road
known locally as Beeley Lane east for 2km. Eventually, when the Hell Bank
Plantation on your left comes to an end, the road will turn in a
south-easterly direction, running straight through open moorland. At this
point (GR: SK287681) you will see a track to your left, where limited parking is available.

After walking along this track for approximately 400m you will come to
the footpath onto the open moorland, as shown on the map and well
marked with 'Chatsworth House Estate' signs. Climb over the prominent
stone stile and follow the main track straight ahead (not the footpath onto
open moorland off to the right) up the gentle slope. As the path begins to
curve round to the right (shown on the OS map) after about 400m, you
should see a rough farmer's track running north (to your right), which will
take you straight to the circle. (This rough farmer's track looked like a temporary feature when we visited.) For a longer walk, Park Gate can be combined with a visit to Hob Hurst's House (see the *Monuments of the Dead*
section for further details).

Details

Park Gate is a relatively well-preserved embanked stone circle located on a
boggy plateau on the moorland above Beeley, at the northern end of a
cairnfield. Overlooked by Harland Edge and Bunker's Hill Wood, it is currently on the edge of a sea of bracken in an area of marshy grass. The two
ringcairns of Beeley Moor North (GR: SK277687) and Beeley Warren North
East (GR: SK279688) are located close by to the north-west.

The circle consists of ten stones in a ring, approximately 12.5m by 12m
in diameter with a further stone, completely buried, to the north-west.
There are four smaller stones on the site, but Barnatt suggests these may
have been part of the kerb rather than actual standing stones. If the stones
were evenly spaced, there may originally have been as many as twenty in
the circle.

The larger stones still present today range between about 0.5m and
0.9m in height, except for one lying to the south, which leans badly and has

all but collapsed. This stone would probably have been well over a metre in height originally and has a possible cupmark on one of its edges. Investigations on the eleventh stone have also revealed that this was also well over a metre tall and would probably have stood as high as the southern stone originally.

The bank, difficult to see in parts, is between 1.5m and 2.5m wide and 15m in diameter. It is clearest to the west and south-west. Within the circle, there is a badly ruined cairn slightly off centre to the south-east. Two further small stones can be found hidden in clumps of grass about 3m from the circle to the west – their origin and purpose are unknown.

Comments

Park Gate is not one of the most well-known circles in the Peak District, but considering its remote location, it does seem to be well-visited; there is evidence of present day fire settings and offerings.

Of particular interest is the possible cupmark on the side of the tallest stone. Further details on prehistoric 'rock art' of this nature are described in detail in the relevant section later in the book. It is unclear whether this circular indentation at Park Gate is an authentic man-made cupmark or whether it is just an intrinsic feature of the stone. However, even if it is natural, it may perhaps have been one of the influencing factors when Bronze Age man chose that particular piece of rock to use in his circle.

Other Sites close by:

Site 14 – The Stanton Moor Group (5 stone circles, Andle Stone, Cork Stone and numerous smaller cairns), **Site 18** – Gibbet Moor North stone circle, **Site 25** – Hob Hurst's House barrow, **Site 26** – Gardom's Edge (Neolithic enclosure, barrow and prehistoric rock art), **Site 35** – Ball Cross hillfort, **Site 36** – Cranes Fort.

References and Further Reading

J. Barnatt "The Stone Circles of the Peak", Turnstone Books, London (1978)

J. Barnatt "The Henges, Stone Circles and Ringcairns of the Peak District", Department of Archaeology and Prehistory, University of Sheffield (1990)

J. Barnatt with contributions from F.M. Chambers "Recent Research at Peak District stone circles including Restoration work at Barbrook II and Hordron Edge, and new fieldwork elsewhere", *DAJ*, volume 116 (1996)

Site 12

Smelting Hill stone circle, Abney Moor, Derbyshire (also known as Abney Moor I)

Map reference: SK203804

Access

Smelting Hill is located on the moor above the village of Abney and is not an easy site to find. Our best route was to turn right off the A625 at Hathersage onto the B6001, drive south for approximately one kilometre where we came to the village of Leadmill. Just after the bridge over the river, we took the first right turn onto a minor road. After following this road for almost 3.5km we parked just before the sign welcoming visitors to the village of Abney.

Having followed our route so far, you will see a footpath on your right (north of the road). Go over the first two stiles and follow the footpath, marked on the map, up through the field, turning right through the gateway. Another stile (quite difficult to climb) will take you onto the moorland path. Continue along here until you reach a crossroads of two footpaths (shown on the OS map). At this point, leave the path and head north into the bracken. Once you have climbed up the slope a little you should see two radio masts – one to the north-west and one to the south-east. Smelting Hill stone circle is placed directly in between the two masts in a grassy area (at the time of writing) free of heather. The solitary remaining standing stone is visible from a distance.

Details

Smelting Hill is an embanked stone circle, now a shadow of its former self, with only two stones remaining to the south-east of the site. One of the stones stands approximately 0.75m in height and again shows signs of weathering, while the other is lying flat. The two are placed approximately 3.5m apart.

The embankment has disappeared in the eastern half of the circle, but can still be faintly traced to the west. This bank would originally have been about 1.5m to 2m wide and circa 11m in diameter.

When the antiquarian, Rooke visited the site, in 1785, four stones were still in place, set at the inner edge of the bank. Rooke noted that when Pegge had investigated the site only fourteen years earlier, there had been nine stones. It is highly likely that the stones were removed when quarrying was carried out nearby.

The two remaining stones of Smelting Hill stone circle

This site at Smelting Hill is often confused with another possible circle, now lost, known as Abney Moor (SK2080). Excavated by Pennington before 1875, when workmen demolished it to build the nearby dry-stone walls, it is described as consisting of a central mound, about 6m in diameter and 1.7m high, surrounded by ten evenly spaced standing stones. Several finds were discovered within, including a human cremation, an urn, a number of amber and jet beads, a leaf-shaped arrowhead and some flakes of flint and chert.

Comments

When we first learnt that there were only two stones remaining at Smelting Hill, we almost decided not to visit, but after discovering it was only a short distance from the road we thought we'd take a look anyway. That proved to be a good decision, for although the circle is now badly ruined, the setting and the atmosphere made our visit well worthwhile.

In a solitary position on the moor, surrounded by bracken and heather, and looking out across the valley to the south, the circle has a certain aura about it. Unlike most of the other sites we have visited, there was no real sign that modern visitors had been there (apart from the local sheep).

The circle is contained in an oasis of grass hidden amongst the heather and bracken, so as with so many sites in the Peak District, it is best visited either earlier or later in the year. We went in May and the vegetation was just beginning to take hold, any later and the going could become difficult.

There is another circle about a kilometre to the east of Smelting Hill. Many sources report that this site, known as Offerton Moor, is also badly ruined. As it is not located close to a road or marked right of way, we decided that it did not warrant a visit for the time being, but for the keen enthusiast, a few details are included below.

Site 13

Offerton Moor stone circle, Derbyshire
(also known as Offerton Moor West)

Map reference: SK213805

Offerton Moor is often referred to as an embanked stone circle, but may possibly be a ringcairn. In his 1990 publication, Barnatt describes the site as consisting of a rubble bank which is 2m to 3.5m wide and has an external diameter of 27m by 23m. Only one visible stone, 'a tiny upright on the inner edge of the bank to the SSE' remains.

A similar site in this area was visited by Pegge in 1761. Described as 'a large circle of stones, some of which stood on end', this is a likely candidate. The stones may have been removed when the dry-stone wall, which stands close by, was constructed.

Other sites close by:

Site 5 – Bamford Moor South stone circle, **Site 8** – The Eyam Moor Group (3 stone circles and barrow), **Site 9** – Froggatt Edge stone circle, **Site 15** – Seven Stones of Hordron Edge stone circle, **Site 16** – Lawrence Field possible stone circle, **Site 29** – Carl Wark hillfort, **Site 31** – Burr Tor hillfort.

References and Further Reading

J. Barnatt "The Stone Circles of the Peak", Turnstone Books, London (1978)

J. Barnatt "The Henges, Stone Circles and Ringcairns of the Peak District", Department of Archaeology and Prehistory, University of Sheffield (1990)

J. Barnatt and K. Smith "Peak District, Landscapes through Time", English Heritage & B.T. Batsford Ltd, London (1997)

Site 14

The Stanton Moor Group

Stanton Moor is an area of partially wooded, sandstone moorland to the west of the river Derwent and south-east of Bakewell. It comprises a Bronze Age cemetery dating to circa 2000BC. The whole moor is littered with over seventy cairns and barrows, five known stone circles (Stanton Moor I, The Nine Ladies (II), Stanton Moor III, IV and Doll Tor) and a number of interesting natural rocky outcrops, the most famous of which being the Cork Stone and the Andle Stone.

Due to the close proximity of so many interesting prehistoric features, the moor is a very popular area and, unfortunately, some of the archaeological sites are beginning to suffer because of its popularity. As a result, English Heritage, the Peak National Park Authority and the landowner are now trying to reverse the damage and preserve this important area for future generations.

In November 2000, exploratory excavations began in the area around the Nine Ladies stone circle to establish what damage was being done to deposits below the ground and to determine how much of the monument still survives from the Bronze Age. Unfortunately, the results of these investigations will not be published in time to be included here, however some observations from a site visit during the excavations are.

Stanton Moor is so richly bestowed with important archaeological sites, that it leaves the visitor spoilt for choice when it comes to accessing them. There are two places to park (marked 'a' and 'b' on our map). From either of these, many of the sites can easily be reached, but to visit all the sites from a single parking area would be tiring if you are walking with young children.

For ease of explanation, we will describe how to get to the sites which are closer to either 'a' or 'b' – feel free to choose differently, but please do so in conjunction with the Ordnance Survey map. Parking point 'a' (GR: SK246641) can be used to reach Stanton Moor I, II (the Nine Ladies), III and IV. Space is limited in the lay-by so park carefully and thoughtfully.

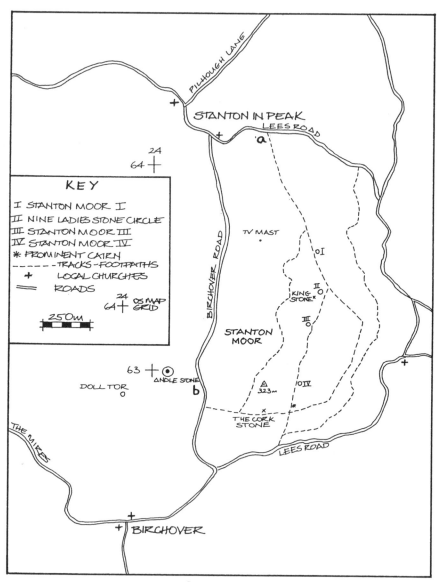

Stanton Moor

Nine Ladies stone circle, Stanton Moor, Derbyshire (also known as Stanton Moor II)

Map reference: SK249635

Access

One of the most well-known sites in Derbyshire, recently much in the media spotlight because of quarrying plans in the area, the Nine Ladies stone circle is signposted from the Lees Road running east from Stanton in Peak. Parking for a limited number of cars is located at GR: SK246642 on the road-side verge (marked on our map as parking point 'a'). From here a marked path leads south from the road initially through a field (along a sandy path) then into a scrubby woodland where you will pass a dark eerie quarried area on the right (very reminiscent of parts of Alderley Edge in Cheshire).

The stone circle is about 800m from the road. The footpaths are generally in good condition (although you may encounter a few sheep along the way) and makes easy walking for young children.

Alternatively, if you want to enjoy a longer walk taking in all the ancient sites of Stanton Moor mentioned here, ending with the Nine Ladies, follow the directions for Stanton Moor III and IV stone circles later in this section.

The Nine Ladies on Stanton Moor, one of the most enigmatic stone circles in the Peak District

Details

Under the guardianship of English Heritage, Nine Ladies is a typical Derbyshire circle consisting of nine visible small standing stones embedded in a grassed over stone rubble bank approximately 11.5m by 10.5m in diameter. The site is the most noticeable example to be found on Stanton Moor.

The stones are all composed of local millstone grit and none are taller than one metre in height. The bank has now all but disappeared, as has the cairn, which once lay in the centre. An interesting discovery was made during the summer of 1976, when the famous drought of that year brought to light a tenth stone which had lain unnoticed for generations beneath the soil.

On our first visit in January 1999, there was one other stone standing slightly off the line of the circle, but upon our return the following month, this modern intruder had been uprooted and lay some distance away on the grass. There may originally have been eleven stones, if they had been evenly spaced out.

As previously mentioned, during November 2000 (at the time of going to press) excavations are being carried out on the monument. At present, we are only able to include information gained during a site visit in the first week of the investigations. Archaeologists are currently examining the area

A picture from Thomas Bateman's 1848 publication showing the Nine Ladies as it was then. The embankment and central cairn are very prominent, illustrating the dramatic erosion that has taken place at the site in just over 150 years.

around the King's Stone (see below) as well as the Nine Ladies. They are cutting an L-shaped trench through the centre of the circle to try to learn more about the rubble bank into which the stones are set, and the central cairn.

This cairn (now almost vanished) has been a matter of discussion for many years, owing to discrepancies between early pictures of the site. A drawing by Rooke in 1782 shows a small cairn in the centre, while in Bateman's 1848 illustration there is clearly a much larger cairn. Archaeologists are hoping to discover whether this cairn dates from the Bronze Age or whether it was just a walker's cairn (a pile of stones built up by visitors in modern times), enlarged over the years. The team is also examining the soil to see if agriculture was taking place in the vicinity of the monuments, but early indications suggest that it was not.

A single standing stone known as the King's Stone or Fiddler's Chair lies approximately 40m to the south-west of the Ladies. Now leaning slightly, the King's Stone is approximately 0.9m in height and has suffered at the hands of a graffiti 'artist'. Local legend says that the circle was formed when nine ladies were turned to stone, punished for dancing on the Sabbath, and that the King's Stone was their fiddler.

For many years the King's Stone has been considered to be an outlier of the circle. Outliers are fairly common at British stone circles and most are

A view of the King's Stone looking back to the Nine Ladies circle

steeped in folklore providing appropriate names. At the Merry Maidens in Cornwall (also known as Dans Maen, meaning 'Dawn's men' or 'stone dance', after girls were again reputedly turned to stone for dancing on the Sabbath) there are the Pipers, a pair of stones lying a quarter of a mile to the north-east. At Stonehenge, the famous 'Heel Stone' is located in the north-east entrance. At the Rollright Stones in Oxfordshire (reputedly representing a king and his army turned to stone by a witch) another 'King's Stone' lies 70m to the north-north-east. At Long Meg and Her Daughters in Cumbria, the outlier 'Long Meg' (said to be a petrified witch of unknown origins) stands an impressive 3.7m high to the south-west.

However, new evidence has now come to light, which may call for a reinterpretation of the King's Stone. In his 1999 article in the *Derbyshire Archaeological Journal*, John Barnatt from the Peak National Park Archaeology Service records that when the site was surveyed in the 1980s, this stone stood within a low, mutilated bank which has since been covered with soil and suffered damage from bonfires. Instead of an outlier it now seems as if the King's Stone could perhaps be part of a ruined stone circle or a ringcairn. At the time of writing, early indications from the 2000 excavations seem to indicate that the King's stone is alone and therefore perhaps an outlier as originally thought. We eagerly await the final decision.

Comments

At first glance the Nine Ladies appears to be a well-preserved example of a stone circle, as all of the stones are clearly visible from a distance and are in relatively good condition. However, upon closer inspection it is clear that the site is suffering serious erosion. The bank and central cairn have all but disappeared, unsuspectingly flattened by the feet of many thousands of visitors each year.

There is evidence of burning at the site, showing that the power of the stones and the sacredness still captivate the hearts of people today. If you visit around the time of the summer solstice ($21^{st} - 22^{nd}$ June) or one of the other pagan festivals, be prepared to meet lots of people. On a visit in June 1999, the surrounding woods were all the colours of the rainbow with numerous tents pitched for the celebrations.

With so many people buried on the moor, it comes as no surprise that a number of strange lights, along with the ghost of a white lady, have been seen in the area. Also of significance is a votive tree, which stands close to the Nine Ladies circle. It is said that anyone wanting a wish to come true should tie a strip of clothing to the tree and repeat their request three times.

Stanton Moor I stone circle, Derbyshire
(also known as Stanton Moor North)

Map reference: SK249637

Access

Located a short distance to the north of the Nine Ladies, Stanton Moor I, now almost completely overgrown by bracken and trees and is very difficult to find.

From the Nine Ladies go back along the path in a north-westerly direction towards the Lees Road. After approximately 200m on your right you will see a dry-stone wall surrounding a field used for sheep grazing. Follow the rough path that runs along the southern boundary of this field for approximately 40m, and then with your back to the dry-stone wall, walk forward for approximately 8m. You should find yourself in the middle of the circle.

Details

Stanton Moor I is the most northerly of the ancient ceremonial sites to be found on the moor and is now very badly ruined and overgrown with vegetation and trees. Originally it was an embanked stone circle with a bank of about 2m wide and 10m by 9m internally in diameter; there were two entrances to the north-north-east and south-south-west.

The circle is now so badly damaged that it cannot be estimated for certain how many stones there would have been originally. Only one of the larger stones, about 0.5m tall, can now be recognised in the undergrowth.

Traces of a mutilated cairn, excavated by Rooke in 1784 can still be seen in the centre. The excavations produced an urn, cremations and a pygmy cup. One such pygmy cup, now housed in the Ashmolean Museum in Oxford, was originally believed to have been found at the Nine Ladies, but could just as easily be the one found here at Stanton Moor I instead. The site was also re-excavated in the 1940s by Heathcote, but the results have never been published.

Comments

Although Stanton Moor I is now almost completely buried in bracken and has mature trees growing on top of it, in some ways it is better preserved than those out on the open moorland. The bank is still quite prominent and its features can be made out under the vegetation. It is probably one of the quietest places on this popular moor, with very few visitors. On our latest visit in November 2000, the site was suffering further damage with some kind of animal burrowing under the embankment.

The Andle Stone, Stanton Moor, Derbyshire (also known as The Oundle Stone)

Map reference: SK241630

Access

The Andle Stone and Doll Tor stone circle are located on the other side of the moor from the Nine Ladies. They are best found by following the Birchover road from Stanton in Peak to Birchover. The Andle Stone can be seen in a field to the right just over a kilometre south of Stanton-in-Peak. Parking is available in a lay-by (GR: SK242628) overlooking the field (marked as parking point 'b' on our map).

Details

Described as a 'huge natural altar', the Andle Stone or Oundle Stone is a dominating outcrop of sandstone, standing alone in the middle of a field, surrounded by a dry-stone wall and a mass of rhododendrons. Approximately 5m high by 4.5m wide, the rock is supposedly carved with ancient cupmarks on the top (although we have not found any written verification

The huge rocky outcrop known as the Andle Stone, standing in a field on Stanton Moor, close to Doll Tor stone circle

of this), modern graffiti, a relatively recent inscription and climbing holes on the sides.

A dedication on the back bears a memorial to the battle feats of Field Marshall Duke of Wellington and Lt. Col. William Thornhill, carved by a man named T. Masters, while a date on the front reads 1758. The Duke of Wellington was, of course, famous for his defeat of Napoleon at Waterloo in 1815. Whilst members of the Thornhill family, one of whom was evidently contemporary with Wellington, were well-known for their mining activities in the Peak District.

Comments

The Andle Stone has obviously been a source of inspiration to people in the area over countless generations and provides a perfect platform to enjoy the extensive local views.

Doll Tor stone circle, Stanton Moor, Derbyshire

Map reference: SK238629

Access

Carry on down the hill past the Andle Stone (on your right) and go through the gap in the field boundary at the bottom. Continue round to the left and you will see a gate leading to a small conifer woodland. Doll Tor is located almost 100m down the grassy path on the left under the trees. You will see the English Heritage signboard on your left.

Details

Maintained by English Heritage and the Peak National Park Authority, Doll Tor is a delightful little stone circle consisting of six standing stones, no more than a metre in height, with an adjoining cairn. Numerous smaller stones litter the woodland around. After Ash Cabin Flat, it is the second smallest circle in Derbyshire.

The circle is approximately 6m by 4.5m in diameter with five stones of similar size and height, and one smaller wider one. It is surrounded on three sides by trees, but there are wonderful views to the west across the valley and hills beyond.

Constructed circa 2000BC to 1500BC, the circle was originally set on the edge of a platform, probably used by the Bronze Age people for seasonal and family ceremonies. A low prehistoric cairn with a central rectangular stone setting was added later at the eastern end of the circle.

The small stone circle of Doll Tor, now restored to look as it would have done
originally in the Bronze Age

Shortly before the spring equinox in 1993 there was an incorrect reconstruction by persons unknown. During this tampering, the circle was
wrongly changed to consist of fourteen standing stones with much of the
eastern cairn removed to form a stone bank over three sides of the cairn's
central setting. Having been recently restored by English Heritage and the
Peak National Park Authority, the site is seen today as it would have been
originally in the Bronze Age.

Doll Tor was first recorded by Thomas Bateman in his *Ten Years' Diggings*, when in 1852 he describes a circle of six stones, two of which had
fallen. Within the space of a mere afternoon, Bateman and his companions
had cleared a space in the centre of the enclosure and discovered a grave
containing three or four cinerary urns and as many cinerary cups. Some of
these are now housed in the Sheffield City Museum.

The site remained forgotten and untouched until local Birchover
archaeologists J.C. Heathcote and his son J.P. Heathcote excavated it
between 1931 and 1933. Beneath a dense mass of grass and heather the
Heathcotes rediscovered the Doll Tor circle and set about further excavations. They discovered both plain and decorated cremation urns containing the remains of adults and children, along with other funerary goods

such as small pieces of unburnt bronze, scrapers and a couple of unusual faience beads, one star shaped and one segmented.

Faience beads, dating to the Early Bronze Age, were made from a glass-like material and were once thought to have originated in distant lands. In fact, Heathcote in his account of the excavations in the *Derbyshire Archaeological Journal*, reports that they may have come from as far away as Egypt. However, in recent years developments in analytical science have led archaeologists to believe that they were made locally in Britain. Nevertheless, they are still an important discovery.

The site of Doll Tor is still regarded as a special place today with visitors leaving many charms and offerings in and around the circle

In total the Heathcotes, whose archaeological finds are housed in a private museum in Birchover, uncovered burials at the base of four of the standing stones as well as a number of others in the cairn mound to the east. It also appears that the damage done in 1993 was not the first time the stones of Doll Tor had suffered at the hands of vandals. Heathcote reports that before excavations in the 1930s were completed, 'three of the standing stones were maliciously damaged by some unknown persons'. Two of the stones were smashed to pieces and had to be cemented back together with 'considerable patience'.

Comments

Doll Tor is a quiet place, hidden away among a small plantation of trees. Depending on the weather and light, the stones can either be set in a sunlit wooded glade or thick 'spooky' woodland. The stones themselves are covered in lichen making them appear a beautiful green colour, very reminiscent of tarnished copper. Judging by the various tokens and charms hidden amongst the stones, the site is still held sacred by many visitors today.

On a cautionary note, visitors should be aware of a hidden deep quarry within twenty metres (to the south-west) of the circle.

The Cork Stone, Stanton Moor, Derbyshire

Map reference: SK245628

Access

If you are combining a visit to Doll Tor with a trip to the other sites around the moor, it is easier to leave your car parked in the lay-by (GR: SK242628) overlooking the Andle Stone (marked as parking point 'b' on our map). Alternatively, there is another lay-by slightly further along the road on the left. A well signposted path leads up onto the moor, but do take care, as first part of this path is constructed from huge boulders which can become slippery when wet. Follow this path up a gentle rise. When you reach the top, you will see the huge Cork Stone just off the path on the left.

Details

The Cork Stone is one of a number of impressive natural outcrops on Stanton Moor. Composed of weathered sandstone it resembles a huge mushroom or cork. As with the Andle Stone it is covered in graffiti from the 19th and 20th centuries and has steps carved into the side to allow access to the top.

The stone was visited by Rooke in 1789 and described as being surrounded by four standing stones 'in a ring around 25 feet' in diameter. There is no sign of these today, but as quarries surround the whole area, it is highly likely that the quarrymen removed these as an easy source of stone.

Other interesting natural outcrops on Stanton Moor include the Cat Stone to the south-east of the tower, the Gorse Stone to the east of Stanton Moor IV and the Heart Stones towards the southern end of the moor.

The weather-worn mushroom of the Cork Stone on Stanton Moor

Stanton Moor IV stone circle/ringcairn, Derbyshire
(also known as Stanton Moor South)

Map reference: SK247629

Access

The fourth stone circle on Stanton Moor is marked on the 1:25000 OS map as an enclosure and if you do not know it is there, it is very easy to miss.

Continue along the path past the Cork Stone, taking the second track off to the left (signposted '9 Ladies half a mile') into an area of more open moorland. You will pass through a Bronze Age cairnfield. A particularly good example of a cairn (marked on the OS map at SK247628) can be seen almost immediately to the right of the path. Stanton Moor IV is about a hundred metres further down the track next to the path on the right-hand side.

Details

Overlooking the gritstone moorlands to the east and south, Stanton Moor IV, although referred to as an embanked stone circle, is more reminiscent of a ringcairn. It is now completely covered in heather, but the egg-shaped ring of the embankment can be seen raised up above the ground and is approximately 12.5m by 13.5m internally in diameter. There appears to be one entrance to the south-west.

A number of small stones survive on the site, including one in the entrance, two at the inner edge of the bank standing 0.35m and 0.6m high, and between one and four other fallen stones. Again, these are difficult to find because of the surrounding vegetation. There may have been as many as eleven originally. There is also a huge depression in the centre (perhaps the result of excavations undertaken by Heathcote in the 1930s and 1940s when six small stones were revealed).

Comments

Stanton Moor IV is probably the least appealing of the named sites on the moor, but if you are travelling past it anyway, it is always worth a quick look. If nothing else, there are picturesque views across the cairnfield and other prehistoric features on the moor.

Stanton Moor III stone circle/ringcairn, Derbyshire (also known as Stanton Moor Central)

Map reference: SK248633

Access

Stanton Moor III is also marked on the OS map as an enclosure. Continue along the main path and just before it enters a wooded area, there is a smaller track off to the left leading to it. (To complete the circuit and go back to where we started from, carry on into the wooded area, and you will come the long way round to the Nine Ladies).

Details

Located on slightly higher ground, Stanton Moor III stone circle (or ringcairn) is very similar to IV, but is much larger and more clearly visible. Only partially overgrown by heather, the egg-shaped bank of stones is approximately 19.5m in diameter. There is, what looks like, a small cairn just off centre, but the interior of the site has been greatly disturbed by rabbits. In fact some years ago a segmented faience bead was found near to one of their burrows.

The circle has two entrances, exactly opposite, to the north and to the south and is the largest on the moor. Both entrances are flanked by stones, the southern one by two stones about 0.5m in height and that to the north by one stone, which is less than 0.5m.

This site was also partially excavated by Heathcote in the 1930s and 1940s when the bank and stones were exposed. It is unclear whether the site ever contained any standing stones, hence the supposition that it is probably a ringcairn. It was visited and sketched by Pegge in the 18th century, but even then no stones were visible.

Other Sites close by:

Site 10 – Nine Stone Close stone circle, **Site 11** – Park Gate stone circle, **Site 21** – Green Low chambered cairn, **Site 24** – Bee Low round cairn, **Site 27** – Rowtor Rocks prehistoric rock art, **Site 33** – Castle Ring hillfort, **Site 34** – Cratcliff Rocks hillfort, **Site 35** – Ball Cross hillfort, **Site 36** – Cranes Fort.

References and Further Reading

J. Barnatt with contributions from F.M. Chambers "Recent Research at Peak District stone circles including Restoration work at Barbrook II and Hordron Edge, and new fieldwork elsewhere", *DAJ*, volume 116 (1996)

J. Barnatt "The Stone Circles of the Peak", Turnstone Books, London (1978)

J. Barnatt "The Henges, Stone Circles and Ringcairns of the Peak District", Department of Archaeology and Prehistory, University of Sheffield (1990)

J. Barnatt "Excavation and Restoration of the Doll Tor stone circle, Stanton, Derbyshire, 1994", *DAJ*, volume 117 (1997)

J. Barnatt and K. Smith "Peak District, Landscapes through Time", English Heritage & B.T. Batsford Ltd, London (1997)

J. Barnatt "Taming the Land: Peak District Farming and Ritual in the Bronze Age", *DAJ*, volume 119 (1999)

T. Bateman "Vestiges of the Antiquities of Derbyshire", London (1848)

A. Burl "A Guide to the stone circles of Britain, Ireland & Brittany", Yale University Press (1995)

J. Cope "The Modern Antiquarian", Thorsons (1998)

J.P. Heathcote "Excavations at barrows on Stanton Moor", *DAJ*, volume 51 (1930)

J.P. Heathcote "Excavations in Derbyshire during 1938" (Report by J.P. Heathcote), *Derbyshire Archaeological and Natural History Society Journal*, volume 59 (1938)

J.P. Heathcote "Excavations at Doll Tor stone circle, Stanton Moor", *DANHSJ*, volume 60 (1939)

J.P. Heathcote "Excavations on Stanton Moor", *DANHSJ*, volume 74 (1954)

J.P. Heathcote "The Nine Ladies stone circle", *DAJ*, volume 100 (1980)

W. Storrs-Fox "Bronze Age Pottery from Stanton Moor", *DAJ*, volume 48/49 (1926/27)

L. Tildesley "Further Excavations on Stanton Moor"; report, *DANHSJ*, volume 57 (1936)

J. Ward "Cinerary Urns and incense cups, Stanton Moor, Derbyshire", *DAJ*, volume 13 (1891)

Site 15

The Seven Stones of Hordron, Moscar Moor, Derbyshire (also known as Hordren Edge)

Map reference: SK215868

Access

The Seven Stones of Hordron are located on Moscar Moor to the east of Ladybower Reservoir and are marked on the Outdoor Leisure Series Dark Peak map. Park in the large lay-by located on the A57 Snake Pass, Manchester to Sheffield road (GR: SK217875). The stone circle is located 600m south of the Cutthroat Bridge on the shelf of land known as Hordron Edge.

Details

Overlooked by Stanage Edge, the Seven Stones of Hordron boast some of the best views in the Peak District. The circle actually consists of nine standing millstone grit stones and one recumbent stone, in a ring about 16m in diameter. In fact, counting all the smaller stones on site, there are twenty-three in total. However, archaeological evidence has revealed that originally there may have been between sixteen and twenty stones.

Unlike most of the other circles in the Peak District, Hordron Edge is a free-standing circle having no embankment. However, all the stones are typically Derbyshire in style, all being less than a metre in height. Again the largest stone stands to the south-west, but here it is only marginally taller than the others. Most of the stones show signs of weathering.

The Seven Stones of Hordron also witnessed tampering by 'persons unknown' in the early 1990s. In 1992 one of the stones, which had previously been buried was re-erected. Following this, John Barnatt, Senior Survey Archaeologist for the Peak National Park Authority, in consultation with English Heritage, re-excavated the area around the new stone and undertook a survey of the whole circle.

It was established that the previously buried stone was covered largely with peat, suggesting it had been covered for some time, perhaps falling in prehistory or deliberately felled in Medieval times when the site was used as a boundary marker. During the 1992 excavation other buried stones, of a similar size to the orthostats, were discovered with between three and five new ones identified.

Examination of the site also showed that it might have been terraced to create a level interior. This procedure is also apparent at other Peak District sites, both embanked and free-standing, including the Nine Ladies and

Stanton Moor III, Bamford Moor South, Barbrook I and Froggatt Edge stone circles.

Comments

The site is very exposed and has a wonderful view throughout 360 degrees. Particularly of interest is Win Hill on the horizon to the south-west. In fact, it has been suggested that the ridges on the top of this stone resemble the hill on the horizon in the background. This stone is sometimes called the Fairy Stone because a number of strange lights have been reported around it.

Win Hill has a companion peak called Lose Hill 3km to the west. Local legend has it that a battle took place between two old English Kings over 1300 years ago. The two warring parties took up residence on the neighbouring hills and battle commenced on the lowlands between. When the moment was right the King of Northumbria's army withdrew up his hill (as they appeared to be losing). The King of Wessex's men saw this as a sign of retreat and chased them hoping to clinch victory. This was a bad move on the southerner's part as pre-gathered boulders and rocks rained down and the King of Northumbria snatched victory. From then on, the tale names the summits Win Hill and Lose Hill. There is no historical evidence to confirm this myth but that has never quashed a good local legend!

Hordron Edge is perhaps the most exposed circle in the Peaks. One Feb-

Hordron Edge during a dramatic spring squall

ruary visit saw us confronted with glorious sunshine accompanied by gale force winds quickly followed by a slushy 'white-out'. This added to the atmosphere of the monument but made for one bitter experience! Again, it is best to visit the site earlier or later in the year, because of the usual summer overgrowth of bracken. Unfortunately the tall, spiky Juncus grass seems to be present all year round and, as with other sites, somewhat obscures the view making it difficult to detect the whole ring.

Other Sites close by:

Site 4 – Ash Cabin Flat stone circle, **Site 5** – Bamford Moor South stone circle, **Site 12** – Smelting Hill stone circle, **Site 13** – Offerton Moor stone circle, **Site 29** – Carl Wark hillfort.

References and Further Reading

W. Anthony "Haunted Derbyshire and the Peak District", Breedon Books Publishing Company, Derby (1997)

J. Barnatt "The Stone Circles of the Peak", Turnstone Books, London (1978)

J. Barnatt "The Henges, Stone Circles and Ringcairns of the Peak District", Department of Archaeology and Prehistory, University of Sheffield (1990)

J. Barnatt with contributions from F.M. Chambers "Recent Research at Peak District stone circles including Restoration work at Barbrook II and Hordron Edge, and new fieldwork elsewhere", *DAJ*, volume 116 (1996)

A. Burl "A Guide to the stone circles of Britain, Ireland & Brittany", Yale University Press (1995)

J. Cope "The Modern Antiquarian", Thorsons (1998)

Site 16

A Possible stone circle: Lawrence Field, Derbyshire

Map reference: SK252797

Access

A possible stone circle is marked on the Ordnance Survey map in Lawrence Field, located immediately to the south of the A625 to the south-east of Hathersage. Parking is available in the 'Surprise View' pay and display car park (GR: SK252801) although this is very popular at the weekend and it is often difficult to find a space. From the car park, you need to go across the main road and follow the footpath to the west of Owler Tor down into Lawrence Field itself.

Details

Although marked on the OS map as a stone circle, there are very few references or details about this site. We searched in the general bracken-covered area for some time, but were only able to find one standing stone which was very reminiscent of stones at other circles in the Peak District.

Hall mentioned a 'druidical circle' in this area in 1853, but no description is given. The only other reference to Lawrence Field that we could find is in John Barnatt's 1990 publication. He describes the site as 'seven to ten small slabs and boulders set at all angles in a 7.5m ring', only four of which were set into the ground and believed it may be nothing more than a fortuitous arrangement of stones.

Other Sites close by:

Site 5 – Bamford Moor South stone circle, **Site 6** – The Barbrook Group (3 stone circles, a barrow, 2 ringcairns and numerous small cairns), **Site 8** – The Eyam Moor Group (3 stone circles and barrow), **Site 9** – Froggatt Edge stone circle, **Site 12** – Smelting Hill stone circle, **Site 13** – Offerton Moor stone circle **Site 17** – Brown Edge stone circle, **Site 26** – Gardom's Edge (Neolithic enclosure, barrow and prehistoric rock art).

References and Further Reading

J. Barnatt "The Henges, Stone Circles and Ringcairns of the Peak District", Department of Archaeology and Prehistory, University of Sheffield (1990)

The ones that got away

Finally there are two other stone circles which, for various reasons, we decided not to visit personally for the purposes of this book. They are both some distance from the road and are referred to as being in ruinous condition. However, in order to make the guide complete, for those keen enthusiasts without small children, brief details are listed below.

Site 17

Brown Edge stone circle, Derbyshire

Map reference: SK288790

Brown Edge stone circle is located on the top of Flask Edge to the west of Totley and a mile to the north-east of Barbrook III. It is situated in an area of access land, but marked on the map as surrounded by several 'danger areas', hence the reason for not making our visit, bearing in mind the safety of our small daughters.

Brown Edge is another example of an embanked stone circle, with an unusually wide bank approximately 3m wide and an external diameter of about 13m. This bank, the inner and outer edges of which were originally surrounded by a low dry-stone wall, appears unusually to have been constructed from clay and burnt turf.

Excavations in 1963 revealed the existence of two stones, both of which had fallen inwards, and a wealth of finds including human cremations (giving radiocarbon dates of 1530BC +/- 150, 1250BC +/-150 and 1050BC +/-150), a pygmy cup, urns, a hearth, a limpet shell and logs that had been burnt on the site. However the archaeologist, Radley, did not reveal whether or not there ever was a full circle of standing stones.

Other Sites close by:

Site 6 – The Barbrook Group (3 stone circles, a barrow, 2 ringcairns and numerous small cairns), **Site 8** – The Eyam Moor Group (3 stone Circles and barrow), **Site 26** – Gardom's Edge (Neolithic enclosure, barrow and prehistoric rock art), **Site 29** – Carl Wark hillfort.

References and Further Reading

J. Barnatt "The Stone Circles of the Peak", Turnstone Books, London (1978)

J. Barnatt "The Henges, Stone Circles and Ringcairns of the Peak District", Department of Archaeology and Prehistory, University of Sheffield (1990)

Site 18

Gibbet Moor North stone circle, Derbyshire

Map reference: SK282708

Gibbet Moor North stone circle is located on the featureless Gibbet Moor, with no footpaths, to the east of Chatsworth House. Discovered in 1985, it is an unusual site consisting of three standing local grit stones that appear to form three corners of a square. The stones, two of which are upright and one of which is leaning, are all just over 0.5m tall.

It has been suggested that this may be a monument known as a 'Four Poster', common in Scotland, but very rare in England, although here there is no evidence for the position of a fourth stone. Barnatt believes that if there was a fourth, all traces have probably been removed by a covering of peat.

A further site on the Moor, known as Gibbet Moor South (GR: SK281702), was also once considered to be a possible stone circle, but after the burning of the surrounding heather, it was confirmed to be a domestic/agricultural site rather than a ritual monument.

Other Sites close by:

Site 6 – The Barbrook Group (3 stone circles, a barrow, 2 ringcairns and numerous small cairns), **Site 11** – Park Gate stone circle, **Site 25** – Hob Hurst's House barrow, **Site 26** – Gardom's Edge (Neolithic enclosure, barrow and prehistoric rock art), **Site 35** – Ball Cross hillfort.

References and Further Reading

J. Barnatt "The Stone Circles of the Peak", Turnstone Books, London (1978)

J. Barnatt "The Henges, Stone Circles and Ringcairns of the Peak District", Department of Archaeology and Prehistory, University of Sheffield (1990)

J. Barnatt with contributions from F.M. Chambers "Recent Research at Peak District stone circles including Restoration work at Barbrook II and Hordron Edge, and new fieldwork elsewhere", *DAJ*, volume 116 (1996)

A. Burl "A Guide to the stone circles of Britain, Ireland & Brittany", Yale University Press (1995)

Lost stone circles

There are several examples of stone circles in Derbyshire, which were mentioned by antiquarians in the recent past and which have now disappeared
entirely on the ground.

The Seven Brideron

The most famous of these lost circles, which had disappeared by the 19th
century, is The Seven Brideron. The site was described by Rooke on a visit
in October 1764 as being located at the south-eastern end of Matlock Moor
and, as the name implies, consisting of a circle of seven stones around 7.5m
in diameter with the tallest stone being over 2m.

However, in recent years a further account by Samuel Pegge has come to
light, suggesting that the circle was actually located at the north-eastern
corner of Matlock Moor, consisted of nine stones rather than seven and was
called the Seven Brethren rather than Brideron. The debate has now ended
as a Boundary Award Map dating to 1779 places the circle around GR:
SK310635, where Pegge said it was.

Top of Riley

Another lost site of some note is known as Top of Riley. Located somewhere on the land between Top Riley and Magclough Farm just over a kilometre to the east of Eyam, the circle was probably destroyed when the area
was enclosed in the 18th and 19th centuries.

The site was visited by Wood in 1842 and referred to in his *History and
Antiquities of Eyam* as 'a collection of a very large circle of stones of high
unhewn pillars, surrounded by a circular ridge of earth. It had an entrance,
if not two'. It may have been an embanked stone circle similar to Wet
Withens. During the 1990s, there were several attempts to try to locate this
circle, but despite searching the whole area, nothing has been found.

In addition to the stone circle, this area also contained a number of other
interesting prehistoric features. Writing in 1848, Thomas Bateman records
that a large urn was found in the Mag Clough, another urn was discovered
when removing an old wall at Riley and in 1828 one previously found at
Riley-side was found to contain weapons and arrowheads of flint. He also
reports that two cairns or barrows on the top of Riley were destroyed many
years previously, in which urns containing ashes and bones were found.

Handsome Cross

A third lost circle, reported by antiquarians, reputedly stood near Handsome Cross on Bradfield Common (GR: SK26?94?). Mentioned by Watson
in 1776 and Hunter in 1819, it has now completely disappeared, probably
suffering yet again at the hands of quarrymen or wall builders in the 19th

century. Watson noted that it consisted of twelve stones in a ring about 8 yards in diameter and possibly had a cairn in the centre.

Woodbrook Quarry

The final known lost site at Woodbrook Quarry (GR: SK285657) is a good illustration that even in the 20th century, when we have come to realise the importance of these prehistoric sites, despite supposed protection by the authorities, destruction still occurs.

Very little is known of the site at Woodbrook Quarry, but it is believed to have been either an embanked stone circle or ringcairn, located on the moorland north-east of Rowsley. It was scheduled as an ancient monument in 1957, but despite this, was destroyed by ploughing and the planting of a forest five years later.

References and Further Reading

J. Barnatt "The Stone Circles of the Peak", Turnstone Books, London (1978)

J. Barnatt "The Henges, Stone Circles and Ringcairns of the Peak District", Department of Archaeology and Prehistory, University of Sheffield (1990)

J. Barnatt with contributions from F.M. Chambers "Recent Research at Peak District stone circles including Restoration work at Barbrook II and Hordron Edge, and new fieldwork elsewhere", *DAJ*, volume 116 (1996)

J. Barnatt "Taming the Land: Peak District Farming and Ritual in the Bronze Age", *DAJ*, volume 119 (1999)

T. Bateman "Vestiges of the Antiquities of Derbyshire", London (1848)

As can be seen from this list, the Peak District is rich in prehistoric archaeology and particularly fortunate in the number of stone circles. The sites vary from very well preserved, such as Barbrook I and Bamford Moor South, to completely lost and destroyed such as Handsome Cross and Woodbrook Quarry. Sadly, none of the sites has remained completely untouched and intact. The last couple of centuries have seen destruction on a major scale, whether from the over enthusiastic digging of antiquarians, local quarrymen and dry-stone wall builders seeking an easy source of stone, or just the sheer weight of visitors to these popular monuments.

Many of the sites are in remote areas and therefore difficult to protect. It is up to us as regular visitors, to play our part in ensuring their survival for generations to come. Remember to be vigilant and report any damage to the relevant agency. Encourage consideration for the stones especially whilst in their presence; and spread the word that these ancient monuments demand not only more recognition but also more respect. They were created by our ancestors and bequeathed to us in the natural process of time, and somewhere along the human chain of evolution they appeared as part of our culture. Let us try to hold them as dear as our ancestors did.

Monuments of the Dead

From the Great Pyramids of Egypt to Silbury Hill in Wiltshire, death has inspired some of the greatest architecture the world over. As one author commented recently 'Tombs are vast, substantial and beautiful, massively constructed from smaller elements to provide an effect of permanence which appears to overcome death'. They are 'not just somewhere to put dead bodies, they are representations of power' (Pearson 1999).

For archaeologists, burials are of great significance because unlike most other finds they were carefully and deliberately placed in the ground. The final resting-place of an individual was specifically chosen and may in some cases have taken months if not years to prepare. Unfortunately, archaeologists are only able to locate a small proportion of the total prehistoric population and most of the funerary rites, which were carried out at the time, will probably always remain a secret. Nevertheless, there is a great deal to be learnt from the bones, grave goods and tombs themselves.

During prehistoric times, the treatment of the dead went way beyond purely providing graves for the departed. Our ancestors invested thousands of man-hours in the construction of large-scale monuments that were to serve both as tombs for the deceased and as a ritual focus for the living. Over the course of 4,000 years, attitudes towards death underwent a series of phases, reflecting the general trends in the culture of the time.

In Neolithic society, individual burials were rare. Instead the bones of certain members of society were carefully sorted and placed collectively together in specially constructed storage places. Elaborate chambered cairns and long barrows predominated as the focus of worship for the community revolved around the veneration of 'the ancestors'. Tombs became more substantial than houses and ambiguously the dead became the centre of life itself. By the Bronze Age, however, the focus had shifted to the individual, with the burial of whole skeletons or cremations occurring in round barrows, in Beaker burials and in urn cemeteries, sometimes accompanied by a wide range of prestige grave goods.

In addition to these funerary monuments, both Neolithic and Bronze Age man also buried their dead in a range of other 'special' places in the landscape. Fragments of human bone along with complete skeletons and cremations are often unearthed at ritual sites such as in the ditches of henges and causewayed enclosures, as well as in the centre, embankments and even under the standing stones of stone circles, perhaps placed there as token votive offerings.

Neolithic burial practice

The earliest structures built to hold the dead were essentially wooden boxes, known as mortuary houses, between 2m and 10m long and placed in a trench or between elongated mounds. Consisting of a rectangular box of wooden planks with a post at each end and a roof, they are often referred to by archaeologists as 'houses of the dead'. Some also had posts creating an elaborate façade and entrance, providing a ritual area where the sacred rites were carried out for the dead. Once they had served their purpose, most were eventually deliberately destroyed by burning and covered with a mound of turf or stones (see long barrows).

Mortuary houses usually contained a pile of human bones carefully selected and placed together rather than whole skeletons. At Whitwell Quarry in the Peak District, one such construction was discovered, with two adjacent wooden structures incorporated into a later cairn. A smaller box was found to contain a number of female bones while the other contained those of a group (Ray, 1999).

During the Early to Middle Neolithic, burials were also placed in caves. Church Dale in Derbyshire provided a rare example where the bones were still located in their original resting-place. In this rock shelter archaeologists have discovered both the complete skeletons of adults and children laid out similar to those found in long barrows (see next section), as well as a group of mixed bones placed in a stone box or cist (Ray, 1999).

Chambered tombs and long barrows

From around 3500BC, mounded structures began to appear in the Neolithic landscape. Essentially, there were two main types, chambered tombs and long barrows. As with the henges of this period, these large-scale monuments required many thousands of man-hours to construct and would have required a great deal of communal co-operation. Again, in the Peak District they are all located in the area of the limestone plateau, where Neolithic man exploited the fertile landscape.

The earliest type of mounded structures were the chambered cairns and chambered barrows consisting of one or more burial chambers, usually constructed from large stone slabs and dry-stone walling with one or more large capstones forming the roof. A mound of earth or stones originally covered the chambers, but at the majority of sites this has been removed or eroded away leaving only bare stones.

In the Peak District, there are eight certain examples of chambered tombs. However, only Five Wells on Taddington Moor (GR: SK123710) has formal public access. Others are Minning Low between Parwich and Elton (GR: SK209572), Green Low at Aldwark (GR: SK232580), Ringham Low near Monyash (GR: SK169664), Bole Hill on Bakewell Moor (GR: SK184676) Harborough Rocks near Brassington (GR: SK243553), Stoney Low near Aldwark (GR: SK218578) and Long Low near Wetton (GR: SK122539). Also included in this chapter is the lonesome monument of the Bridestones on the Cheshire/Staffordshire border (GR: SJ906662), because although it is not actually in the Peak District, we feel it is close enough and important enough to warrant inclusion.

The chamber at West Kennet long barrow in Wiltshire, giving an idea of how the chambered tombs such as the Bridestones once looked

The second type of Later Neolithic monument was the unchambered long barrow. Consisting of a rectangular or trapezoidal mound ranging between 20m and 120m long and 1m and 7m high, they were usually orientated east to west. In the south of England, in areas generally lacking in stone, long barrows were mostly constructed from earth, whereas in the north they were often made from stone and thus, strictly speaking, should be called long cairns. The bones of the dead, both jointed (articulated) and disjointed (disarticulated), were usually placed on the floor of these structures and rarely had grave goods associated with them.

Excavations have revealed that the barrow mounds originally covered timber structures (mortuary houses) and that some had spectacular facades and forecourts. These acted as a ceremonial focus for the local community, perhaps as shrines where the ancestors were worshipped. Areas of burning and pits containing food remains and pottery are often found in these fore-courts as well as the ditches, perhaps indicating that sacred rituals were enacted there.

As previously mentioned, these Neolithic monuments were almost certainly used for the storage of specific bones for ritual purposes (usually the skulls and long bones), rather than for the interment of whole bodies. Only rarely do excavations reveal complete skeletons. More commonly archaeologists are presented with a jumble of bones often showing characteristic signs of weathering, indicating that the bodies of many individuals were first exposed to the elements until the flesh decomposed, perhaps in mortuary houses or on excarnation platforms.

One such platform, possibly the only certain example in the UK, was discovered a few years ago at Stoney Middleton in Derbyshire, when English Heritage were excavating two decaying Bronze Age barrows in a ravine known as Longstone Rake. Lying beneath one of the barrows, archaeologists discovered the platform littered with hundreds of human teeth and bones and were confident that it dated to circa 3000BC. Evidence indicated that the site had remained in use for over a thousand years and that the platform itself was enclosed by a limestone, rubble wall with an entrance formed by three standing stones (3rd Stone, Spring 1997; Barnatt, 1999).

Often in long barrows, the condition of the bones varies from badly eroded to a relatively good condition, suggesting that these monuments may have been in use for several generations. As to who was chosen to receive such a burial, we can only guess. Sometimes, only a few individuals are discovered, suggesting perhaps only the elite members of a society were selected, while others contained hundreds of bones and must certainly have been communal burial vaults.

Neolithic grave goods

Both in the Neolithic chambered tombs and with most Early Bronze Age burials, individuals were accompanied to the next world by a range of personal effects. These may have belonged to the person during life or may have been gifts from the mourners to assist in the afterlife and thus prevent the dead from haunting the living. Some items discovered show signs of wear and were obviously used in life, while others were specifically made for burial. On occasion, the grave goods were deliberately ritually broken before burial, leaving only shards of pottery and flint flakes, perhaps so that the 'spirit' of the object might also go to the next world.

The most common type of grave goods found in association with Neolithic burials are animal bones, and flint and stone tools, including axes, leaf-shaped and barbed and tanged arrowheads, scrapers, knives and stone wristguards worn by archers to protect their arms. Pots and bowls are also common.

Neolithic pottery generally falls into three distinct categories, enabling archaeologists to ascertain approximately what phase a burial occurred in. The earliest known Neolithic pottery dating from circa 3300BC onwards is characteristically plain, fine and hard with a round base, sometimes burnished and tempered with grit. There are several regional varieties, of which Grimston ware has often been found in the Peak District.

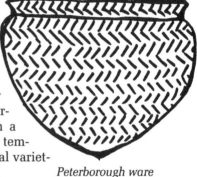

Peterborough ware

Following this came Peterborough ware, a coarse, thick, round-bottomed pottery profusely decorated with a range of designs using stamps, combs, cord, fingers and bird bones. This in turn eventually gave way to Grooved ware (circa 3000-2000BC), a flat-bottomed, bucket or flower-pot shaped pottery, which was characteristically thick and decorated with grooved lines. Just how

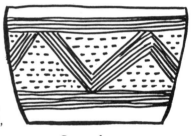

Grooved ware

far these ceramic phases overlapped is a topic of much discussion.

The Beaker Phenomenon

From around 2500BC onwards, following increased trade with the Continent, a new phase of burial practice reached the British Isles. Often referred to as the 'Beaker phenomenon', this development was named after a new kind of pottery drinking cup and characterised by burials with an accompaniment of rich grave goods. Beaker ware was a characteristically fine, thin-walled, well-fired drinking vessel, usually red in colour and covered with various zones of complicated geometric decoration over the majority of the exterior surface. Some had handles and a pattern inlaid with a special white paste.

Beaker ware

The Beaker burials themselves usually consisted of a single crouched inhumation or cremation, covered by a small barrow or cairn, placed in a flat grave or as a secondary interment in a Neolithic long barrow. Some archaeologists believe that this positioning of the skeleton in what is also known as the 'foetal position', may represent a belief in rebirth. A study carried out on Beaker burials in Yorkshire has revealed that the males were normally placed on their left side with their heads to the east, while the females were placed on their right side with heads to the west (Ray, 1999).

In the Peak District, the principal area of Beaker activity was concentrated around the barrow rich area to the south-east of Arbor Low, with a second group close to Hind Low, south of Buxton. It is interesting to note that although there are many Beaker burials in close proximity to Arbor Low, there is a marked absence of barrows containing beakers actually within the confines of the monument complex itself. The barrow in the bank of the henge contained burials with Food Vessels, i.e. coarse, thick, flat based pots with a decorated shoulder and rim, which are generally contemporary with but also extending later in date than Beakers.

As previously mentioned, as well as being accompanied by distinctive pottery drinking cups, the Beaker burials usually also contained a variety of prestigious grave goods. By the time of the Beaker culture, copper objects and copper working had been introduced to the British Isles, but stone implements continued to be deposited with burials for several hundred years. As in the Neolithic, flint daggers, arrowheads, scrapers, stone maceheads, battle-axes and wristguards accompanied the dead on their journey to the next world. Only from circa 2000BC did bronze objects begin to appear.

Other personal belongings commonly found during the Beaker phase are those made from bone and antler including belt rings, fasteners, pendants, combs, buttons, beads and pins. Shale and jet objects such as beads, buttons, belt-rings and pendants were also common, as were faience beads, like those discovered at Doll Tor stone circle (site 14). Food and drink may also have been included. A Beaker pot discovered recently in Scotland was found to have contained honeyed mead.

Bronze Age burial rites

During the late Neolithic period chambered tombs, which had been in use for centuries, were suddenly abandoned. The chambers were carefully blocked off and the facades closed. By the Early Bronze Age, the most notable type of funerary monument was the round barrow. As the ritual focus of the monuments for the living shifted from the large henge monuments to the smaller localised stone circles, so those of the dead moved from the communal chambered cairns and long barrows to smaller, family-orientated round barrows and cairns.

There are over 500 examples of round barrows in the Peak District the most well-known of which being Gib Hill near Arbor Low, described in an earlier chapter (site 1). In general, Peak District round barrows range in size up to about 30m across and mainly survive as grass covered mounds. Thomas Bateman and Samuel Carrington excavated many of these sites in the 1840s and 50s. They opened over 400 barrows in the southern Pennine region, mainly on the limestone plateau where due to the alkaline soils the bones were better preserved. Very few have been opened in modern times however.

To mention all the barrows in the Peak District would be a book in itself, so in the following pages there are just a few notable examples, illustrating the trend in general. For those wishing to research the subject further, the two books by Thomas Bateman, *Vestiges of the Antiquities of Derbyshire* (1848), and *Ten Years' Diggings in Celtic and Saxon Grave Hills in the Counties of Derby, Stafford and York* (1861) provide a great deal of in depth information on the individual sites. In addition, John Barnatt of the Peak National Park Authority compiled a 'barrow corpus' in the early 1990s but the number of sites is being constantly updated as the Park Authority's Archaeology Service is systematically searching for new sites. Only about a quarter of the Park has been surveyed so far and, therefore, new barrows are being found every year (Barnatt, 1999).

The most common type of Bronze Age barrow in Britain is the bowl barrow, consisting of a simple round mound (again either of earth or stone), surrounded by a ditch. Inside the mound the burial, which could be an

Gib Hill near Arbor Low where a Bronze Age round barrow was superimposed on top of a Neolithic long barrow

inhumation or cremation, was placed either in a pit lined with stone slabs (cist) or wood, in a rock cut grave, on the land surface itself, on wooden planks or even in a wooden coffin. The mounds were often enlarged over time. In fact, some of the Earlier Neolithic long barrows had round barrows superimposed at one end. Again, Gib Hill near Arbor Low is a good example.

In the British Isles in general, archaeologists believe that round barrows, unlike long barrows, were specifically constructed for the burial of one high status individual, usually a male, although there are a few examples containing burials of females and infants. However in the Peak District, archaeological evidence confirms that the round barrows contained several primary burials of people of both sexes and all ages. In some cases, the monuments were used for about a thousand years (circa 2500 to 1500BC) with between five and twenty-five individuals buried within.

It has been estimated that during the thousand or so years the barrows were in use, on average less than one individual per generation was interred within. Therefore, they could not have been used for the burial of the elite members of society, as there would have been considerably more than one burial per generation. Some believe that like the stone circles, the round barrows were designed to be territorial markers, portraying individual family claims on the land. Perhaps originally constructed by the first settlers to represent the community as a whole and then added to with later interments during times of trouble to reinforce land ownership (Barnatt & Smith, 1997). The only known exception is the round barrow within the henge bank at Arbor Low, which was undoubtedly constructed as a status symbol for the burial of an elite member of society.

Cremation cemeteries and cairnfields

By 1700BC Bronze Age burial custom was entering another phase with cremation becoming the more predominant form of practice. Corpses were burnt on huge wooden pyres to leave only small fragments of bone, a proportion of which was carefully collected from the ashes of the pyre. The personal belongings of the deceased were either destroyed by the flames or buried whole with the remains.

Cinerary urns were common, either containing cremated bones themselves or accompanying inhumations, both as primary or secondary burials in a barrow or, as was prevalent in northern Britain, in flat cremation cemeteries. The most common type of urn was the collared urn, a heavy coarse pot with a variable cover of decoration. The Heathcotes unearthed many of these on Stanton Moor (site 14). In addition, miniature cups, known as pygmy cups frequently accompanied cremations in urns. Often perforated with one or more holes, they are generally accepted to be an 'accessory ves-

Bronze Age Cinerary Urns from Stanton Moor (Derbyshire County Council: Buxton Museum and Art Gallery)

sel', which probably had some kind of ritual function, perhaps holding incense. However, in one case a pygmy cup was found to contain the cremated bones of a baby and may perhaps have been interred with its mother who died in childbirth (Grinsell, 1953). By circa 1400BC, the urns had become very plain and were poorly fired, suggesting they were made in a hurry and therefore meant purely for funerary purposes.

The majority of burials discovered in the Bronze Age are those found in the barrows, built both on the limestone plateau and on the gritstone moorlands. As for those not interred in such monuments, we rarely get to glimpse their final resting-places, as they are very difficult to locate. Burials of this type are more apparent in the upland areas where, as previously mentioned, archaeological evidence from field systems has revealed that each family had its own ritual monuments for the living and the dead. As well as the larger barrows, a number of smaller cairns are often found in these areas, many containing human cremations. It would make sense for the early farmers clearing the land to put the stone to a practical use, but the act of burying the dead in their fields may also have had some kind of symbolic significance, perhaps restoring fertility to the soil.

Elsewhere burial occurred in flat cremation cemeteries, but these are

One of the numerous burial cairns on Big Moor

incredibly hard to find, as they leave no obvious trace on the surface. Two such cemeteries have been discovered completely by chance in Derbyshire. In the 1920s, quarrymen working at the south-western end of Stanton Moor unearthed a number of cremations unaccompanied by urns, while in the 1980s workmen cutting a drain on Eaglestone Flat near Baslow discovered a similar cemetery (Barnatt & Smith, 1997).

By circa 1000BC, urn cemeteries had fallen out of use and as far as archaeologists can tell there was an absence of formal burial rites until inhumation cemeteries became common in the Later Iron Age. It has been suggested that as the worship focus shifted from the large-scale monuments to water and woodland, so perhaps did the burial practice, with bodies interred in watery locations.

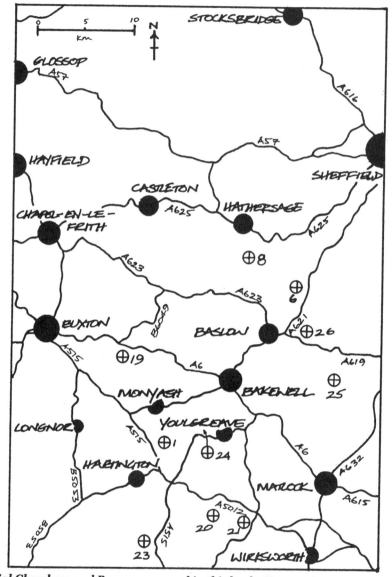

Burial Chambers and Barrows covered in this book. Site 1: *Arbor Low Barrow and Gib Hill Barrows.* **Site 6:** *Barbrook Barrow.* **Site 8 :** *Eyam Moor Barrow.*
Site 19: *Five Wells Chambered Cairn.* **Site 20:** *Minning Low Chambered Round Cairn.* **Site 21:** *Green Low Chambered Cairn.* **Site 23:** *Green Low Round Barrow.* **Site 24:** *Bee Low Round Cairn.* **Site 25:** *Hob Hurst's House Barrow.*
Site 26: *Three Men of Gardom's Barrow*

Neolithic chambered tombs and long barrows

Site 19

Five Wells chambered cairn, Taddington Moor, Derbyshire

Map reference: SK124711

Access

From the A515 (Buxton to Ashbourne road) turn onto the A5270, known locally as Old Coalpit Lane, signposted to Chelmorton. After approximately 1.5km, when the road takes a right angle to the left, follow the road straight ahead known locally as 'The Ditch'. After approximately 2km you will come to a crossroads where you should turn left onto Moor Lane. After about 0.5km where this road bears off to the right, you will see Pillwell Lane leading to Fivewells Farm. Park at the bottom of the lane. A short walk along the track will bring you to a signposted path running east to the burial chamber. The hilltop is very exposed so make sure you are well protected against the elements.

Five Wells chambered tomb as it stands today

Details

Reputed to be the highest megalithic tomb in Britain, Five Wells chambered cairn stands on the false crest of a limestone plateau, 427m (1400ft) high on Taddington Moor, overlooking the fertile Wye valley. The chambered cairn is now a shadow of its former self after the mound was removed by wall builders around 200 years ago and after extensive excavation yet again

The passage tomb of Bryn Celli Ddu on Anglesey, giving an idea of how Five Wells may have looked originally

by the local antiquarian Thomas Bateman in 1846. Only one of the chambers is still fully standing.

Created in the Neolithic period circa 4500BC to 2000BC, Five Wells would originally have comprised two chambers constructed from large limestone slabs backing onto each other. These inner chambers were accessed via two low entrances facing east and west, with a dry-stone wall to either side and covered with a circular mound of earth.

Three excavations took place at Five Wells in the 19th century, some of the finds from which can be seen in the Buxton Museum, along with a reconstruction of how the chamber would once have looked. The first excavation happened on the 25th August 1846 when in his usual day's work Thomas Bateman discovered a number of human bones of both sexes, the jawbones of twelve individuals and a flint arrowhead.

In 1865, a Francis Lukis investigated the western passage, where he unearthed two or three decaying skeletons along with animal teeth, both Early and Late Neolithic pottery and a Neolithic arrowhead. He also discovered two Early Bronze Age flint artefacts, but did not record where exactly on the site these came from. In addition, Lukis uncovered two stone cists which had been inserted after the mound was constructed, one just north of the centre containing a skeleton and burnt bone and another north of the west entrance passage against the original outer edge of the mound. This second cist also contained a skeleton and a flake of flint.

Finally from 1899 to 1901, Micah Salt, a self taught archaeologist from Macclesfield in Cheshire, investigated the site. He discovered pottery fragments of Peterborough and Grimston ware both inside and outside the chambers.

Comments

Carefully sited in a place with commanding views over the once unspoilt Wye valley and beyond, the tomb of Five Wells was almost certainly designed as a special place where the bones of 'the ancestors' could be kept and periodically brought out for ceremonies and rituals. When first constructed the newly hewn white limestone must have been very striking. Sadly, the A6 running below and the neighbouring landfill site now spoil the views.

Nowadays, the chamber provides a welcoming respite from the elements for visitors, but it must once have been quite a frightening place for those chosen to crawl down into the eerie depths of the dark chamber to retrieve the bones of those long departed from this world.

Other Sites close by:

Site 2 – Staden earthworks, **Site 32** – Fin Cop hillfort.

References and Further Reading

J. Barnatt and K. Smith "Peak District, Landscapes through Time", English Heritage & B.T. Batsford Ltd, London (1997)

T. Bateman "Vestiges of the Antiquities of Derbyshire", London (1848)

J. Cope "The Modern Antiquarian", Thorsons (1998)

L.V. Grinsell "The Ancient Burial Mounds of England", Methuen & Co, London (1953)

C.R. Hart "The North Derbyshire Archaeological Survey", North Derbyshire Archaeological Trust, Chesterfield (1981)

Site 20

Minning Low chambered cairn, near Aldwark, Derbyshire

Map reference: SK209573

Details

Minning Low is the largest and most prominently sited cairn in the Peak District, 2km to the west of Aldwark. Surrounded by a beech plantation 500m to the east of The High Peak Trail between the villages of Parwich and Elton, it is a landmark for miles around. Measuring 34m by 44m, the cairn consists of at least four chambers and has undergone a number of construction phases.

The Low originally began life as a single chamber with a small mound comprised mainly of limestone probably during the Neolithic period. It was later covered by a long cairn with four chambers and later still converted into a massive circular mound, perhaps during the Bronze Age.

Several of the burial chambers in the region were opened as early as the Roman period when looting became fashionable as the Romano-British villa owners went in search of curios to decorate their houses. Evidence suggests that Minning Low may have been one of these for when Thomas Bateman excavated the site in the 1840s and 1850s, as well as finding a human skeleton he also discovered Roman pottery and coins, dating from the 4th century AD. This should come as no surprise because the main Roman road, which ran from Buxton to Carsington within a few hundred metres of Arbor Low, also went straight past Minning Low.

By the early 1970s, following Bateman's excavations and earlier robbing by wall builders in the 18th century, the site was in such a dilapidated state that it was decided to carry out work to clear out the rubble. In 1973 and 1974 Barry Marsden undertook investigations in all four of the chambers. Having been greatly disturbed and robbed in the past, the main aim was to establish how each chamber was constructed. However the excavations did produced a small amount of finds including a few fragments of Beaker ware, numerous shards of Romano-British pottery, several adult and human bones, part of an Early Bronze Age bronze ear-ring and nine bronze Roman coins most of which dated to the 4th century AD.

A further excavation by persons unknown was undertaken in 1978 to 1979. They dug beneath the passage walls and in two of the chambers, leaving the monument in such a dangerous state that it had to be filled with quarry waste to prevent collapse.

Other Sites close by:

Site 10 – Nine Stone Close stone circle, **Site 21** – Green Low chambered cairn, **Site 23** – Green Low round barrow, **Site 27** – Rowtor Rocks prehistoric rock art, **Site 33** – Castle Ring hillfort, **Site 34** – Cratcliff Rocks hillfort.

References and Further Reading

T. Bateman "Vestiges of the Antiquities of Derbyshire", London (1848)

L.V. Grinsell "The Ancient Burial Mounds of England", Methuen & Co, London (1953)

C.R. Hart "The North Derbyshire Archaeological Survey", North Derbyshire Archaeological Trust, Chesterfield (1981)

T.G. Manby "Chambered Tombs of Derbyshire", *DAJ*, volume 78 (1958)

B. Marsden "Excavations at the Minning Low Chambered Cairn, (Ballidon I), Ballidon, Derbyshire", *DAJ*, volume 102 (1982)

Site 21

Green Low chambered round cairn, Aldwark, Derbyshire

Map reference: SK232580

Details

The Neolithic tomb of Green Low (not to be confused with Green Low Bronze Age round barrow on Alsop Moor at SK151554) is sited on the top of a ridge close to the village of Aldwark, 2km to the east of Minning Low. Although it is located near to a footpath, the chambered tomb itself is actually on private land.

Green Low consists of a robbed round cairn with an exposed chamber and passage entered via a forecourt at the southern end of the mound. Located at an elevation of 311m (1020ft) on a gorge that runs east to the river Derwent, the tomb commands spectacular views to the north, east and south-west, overlooking Harborough Rocks and Minning Low.

Thomas Bateman excavated the site on the afternoon of 19th July 1843. He noted that the cairn had already been much disturbed with the upper part of the mound having largely been removed, leaving exposed the stones of the chamber. Composed of limestone it was divided into two compartments. Bateman and his team set about removing the soil from within the chamber. In one of the cists, they discovered a badly damaged human skeleton along with a piece of 'slatestone' and the fragments of two urns. In the other compartment were a few human teeth and a large number of animal bones, including those of a horse and a dog.

T.G. Manby carried out further excavations in 1963 and 1964, sponsored by the Derbyshire Archaeological Society. In the layer of soil covering what was left of the cairn material, he discovered the bones of sheep and oxen, a few human bones, quartz pebbles, flint flakes and Roman pottery and coins dating to the 4th century AD when the tomb had been interfered with. In the cairn itself he uncovered a well-preserved skull and jawbone with a badly fractured skeleton and other human bones and teeth along with those of pig, dog, sheep and red deer. Several pieces of Beaker pottery found here enabled him to date the site to the second half of the third millennium BC in the Late Neolithic.

Manby's excavations also revealed that the tomb had been deliberately blocked, with the entrance closed and the paved limestone forecourt filled in. A closing slab, held in place with a wedge-shaped stone, rested in a slot between the paving stones while a number of horizontally lain slabs blocked the entrance. In the forecourt beneath the blocking material a large number of burnt quartz pebbles, pieces of prehistoric pottery and yet more bone from humans, pigs, sheep, goats and oxen were unearthed.

The list of archaeological finds above may sound like the remains of a Neolithic rubbish pit, but when examined more closely they provide a wealth of information about ancient burial customs. Imagine an individual in the community dies and, for some reason, they are chosen to receive burial in a specially constructed tomb that has taken months to build. Their body, perhaps whole or perhaps only a skeleton, is laid to rest inside the dark chamber alongside the bones of their long-dead ancestors. Accompanying them on their journey to the next world is a range of personal possessions. They are provided with food (pork, lamb, goat and oxen) and drink in an ornate pottery Beaker, flint both in the form of tools and as a raw material to help them light a fire for cooking and warmth, quartz pebble charms to ward off evil and maybe even their faithful hunting dog.

After the death rites have been performed, the mourners seal up the tomb and give the deceased a proper send off. Fires are lit in the forecourt and a huge feast of deer, oxen, pork, lamb and goat is prepared. Once stripped of their meat, the bones are discarded among the ashes of the fire. As a final tribute, a toast is made with a cup of drink ritually broken at the entrance, leaving scattered fragments of pottery for archaeologists to find some 4,500 years later.

Other Sites close by:

Site 10 – Nine Stone Close stone circle, **Site 14** – The Stanton Moor Group (5 stone circles, Andle Stone, Cork Stone and numerous smaller cairns), **Site 20** – Minning Low chambered round cairn, **Site 27** – Rowtor Rocks prehistoric rock art, **Site 33** – Castle Ring hillfort, **Site 34** – Cratcliff Rocks hillfort.

References and Further Reading

T. Bateman "Vestiges of the Antiquities of Derbyshire", London (1848)

L.V. Grinsell "The Ancient Burial Mounds of England", Methuen & Co, London (1953)

C.R. Hart "The North Derbyshire Archaeological Survey", North Derbyshire Archaeological Trust, Chesterfield (1981)

T.G. Manby "Chambered Tombs of Derbyshire", *DAJ*, volume 78 (1958)

T.G. Manby "The Excavation of Green Low Chambered Tomb", *DAJ*, volume 85 (1965)

Site 22

The Bridestones chambered long barrow, near Congleton, Cheshire-Staffordshire Border

Map reference: SJ906662

Access

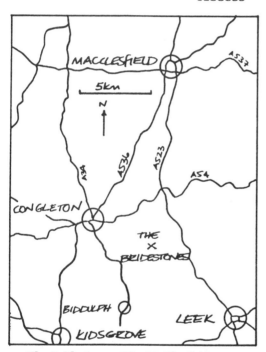

The Bridestones burial chamber is located on the Cheshire/Staffordshire border, near Congleton. It can be found just off the country lane which links the A523 (Macclesfield to Leek road) to the A527 (Congleton to Biddulph road), known locally as Dial Lane.

Parking is available on the roadside verge and the stones are reached by taking a short walk along the drive leading to Bridestones Farm. The monument can be found to the left in a small fenced area through the wooden gate. Please note that the drive ahead is private land.

The Bridestones. Site 22: The Bridestones Chambered Long Barrow

Details

Often described as an 'outlier of the Neolithic monuments of the White Peak', the Bridestones is an ancient burial chamber. Legend has it that it was dedicated to the goddess Bridgit or Bride and that it is thought to be closely connected with ancient fertility rights.

Located between the hillside of Bosley Cloud and Wolfe Lowe, the burial chamber is now a shadow of its former self with thousands of tons of stone having been taken by the builders of the nearby turnpike road in

1764. Other stones were taken to build the adjacent house and farm, while yet more were recycled into an ornamental garden in Tunstall Park.

Anyone reading about the history of this burial monument will come across a variety of theories as to how the Bridestones may once have looked. It now seems almost certain that the stones formed a chambered long barrow or cairn dating to the Neolithic period, perhaps looking similar to West Kennet in Wiltshire.

It has been estimated that the mound of stones originally covering the Bridestones encompassed an area of about 110m by 11m. The burial chamber inside the barrow was divided into two smaller compartments, only one of which now survives. Separating these two chambers was a stone with a hole in. As at Green Low chambered cairn, there was also a forecourt where ritual practices were carried out.

Today, only a few remaining megaliths greet visitors. Two large standing stones, both 2.5m or more, stand slightly offset at the entrance to the surviving burial chamber. There would almost certainly have been two similar stones on the other side of the entrance originally. Upon close inspection, you can see that the tallest of these stones has been cemented back together at some time in the recent past.

The chamber itself is approximately 6m long by 2m wide, consisting of three large stones approximately 1.5m tall on each of the flanks, a larger standing stone (about 1.8m) at the far end, and a smaller flatter stone in the entrance. The side stones, now split into three pieces were originally believed to have been one large piece.

There are several other stones of significance on site, but these can be difficult to see if the bracken is high. A large amount of stone

The few remaining stones of the Bridestones, once a huge chambered long barrow

The stones in the wall of the driveway to Bridestones Farm closely resemble those of the Bridestones

material matching that of the monument is also very noticeable in the wall running alongside the drive to the farm.

The site is discussed in several historical accounts, highlighting its demise in recent centuries. In his book, *Scientific Rambles Round Macclesfield* published in 1878, J.D. Sainter, amateur archaeologist, geologist and natural historian refers to an earlier account of the Bridestones from 1766 when it appears there were several more stones forming a circle close to the chamber:

'There are six or eight upright stones, from three to six feet broad, of various heights and shapes, fixed about six feet from each other in a semicircular form, and two stones where the earth is very black from being mixed with ashes of oak-charcoal. It is apprehended that the circle was originally complete and 27 feet in diameter, for there is the appearance of holes where stones have been; and also of two single stones, one standing east of the circle at about five or six yards difference, and the other at the same distance from that'.

In the following years several of the stones were removed and an account from 1854 describes the site much as it appears today. The author, who is not mentioned by Sainter, records that 'of the semicircle of six stones standing immediately east of the cistavern, none remain; but one is thrown down. The two now standing at the eastern angle of the stone chest are much as they were a century ago – one is full height and the other broken off'.

Comments

Unless you have visited somewhere like West Kennet, it is very hard to imagine how the barrow must once have looked. Now fenced off in the corner of a field surrounded by yews, rhododendrons and conifers, within a hundred metres or so of the country lane, the Bridestones has sadly lost much of its former impressiveness. Nevertheless, for those who take the time have a closer look, the importance of the site soon becomes apparent.

References and Further Reading

A. Crosby "A History of Cheshire", Phillimore & Co. Ltd, Chichester (1996)

L.V. Grinsell "The Ancient Burial Mounds of England", Methuen & Co, London (1953)

H.J. Higham "The Origins of Cheshire", Manchester University Press (1993)

J.D. Sainter, "Scientific Rambles Round Macclesfield", Silk Press reprint, Macclesfield (1999)

Bronze Age round barrows and cairns

The majority of the most accessible Bronze Age round barrows and cairns have been mentioned in earlier chapters both in association with the henges and stone circles. These include Eyam Moor barrow near Wet Withens Stone Circle (Site 8, GR: SK225790), the barrow near Barbrook I (Site 6, GR: SK279756), the round barrow in the henge bank of Arbor Low itself (Site 1, GR: SK160636) and Gib Hill close by (Site 1, GR: SK158634). As previously mentioned there are hundreds of round barrows in the Peak District, so to include them all would be a book in itself. We have therefore chosen to cover only a select few, which for one reason or another have gained much notoriety.

Site 23

Green Low round barrow, Alsop Moor, Derbyshire

Map reference: SK151554

Access

A short walk is necessary if you want to visit the nettle covered bump that is now Green Low round barrow. We found that the easiest route to the site was to park at the old Alsop Station, now a pay and display car park (GR: SK156548) on the popular Tissington Trail. From here, take the Trail north for 0.5km until a footpath leaves the trail and goes down the embankment to the left (west). The barrow is located 200m to the north-west behind a dry-stone wall, but please be aware this is on private land.

Details

Located on an elevated piece of land to the west of the A515 Buxton to Ashbourne road, Green Low is a highly important Bronze Age round barrow which was found to contain a Beaker burial accompanied by a large collection of prestige grave goods.

The highly ornamented Beaker and weapons found by Bateman at Green Low in 1845 (Bateman 1848)

The site was first excavated by Thomas Bateman on the afternoon of the 25th April, 1845. Inside the mound, Bateman discovered a cist containing a skeleton in a crouched position along with 'an elegant and most elaborately-ornamented drinking cup, a piece of spherical pyrites. . . a flint instrument of circular-headed form, and a splendid flint dagger'. Lower down the back of the skeleton he uncovered three flint barbed arrowheads, seven other flint tools and 'three instruments made from the ribs of some animal, neatly rounded at each end', perhaps, as Bateman suggests, these were modelling tools used in the construction of urns or maybe the remnants of primitive bows. The remains of an infant lay close to the pelvis while across the pelvis itself a bone pin was found. This was probably used to secure the wrappings of a shroud.

In 1963, the site was re-excavated by Barry Marsden. In the cairn material, he unearthed several fragments of Romano-British pottery along with a number of flint flakes, quartz pebbles, the canine tooth of a child, two teeth of a long-horned ox, various teeth from a horse, a red deer and a fox, and bones from a raven and some sheep.

The soil around the area of the grave pit disturbed by Bateman, yielded a number of finds including a fine knife of blue-grey flint which showed signs of wear, proving it had been used, and a menagerie of animal bones including the wishbone of a mallard duck. In the grave pit itself Marsden discovered the remains of a skeleton with the bones carefully piled as Bateman had left them.

Comments

At first sight, this barrow is unimpressive due to its overgrown condition, agricultural location and close proximity to a dry-stone wall. However, the artefacts discovered by both Bateman and Marsden show just how important the barrow once was. This importance is reflected in its location. To the east, Green Low has panoramic views towards the heart of the Derbyshire Dales (although now interrupted by the redundant railway line which is the Tissington Trail today). To the west, it takes in splendid views over several dales including Dove Dale, Mill Dale and Hall Dale. This would undoubtedly have been a prestigious location for a prestigious burial.

Other Sites close by:

Site 20 – Minning Low chambered round cairn.

References and Further Reading:

T. Bateman "Vestiges of the Antiquities of Derbyshire", London (1848)

B. Marsden "The re-excavation of Green Low – A Bronze Age Round Barrow on Alsop Moor, Derbyshire", *DAJ*, volume 83 (1963)

Site 24

Bee Low round cairn, near Youlgreave, Derbyshire

Map reference: SK192648

Details

Bee Low is a large Bronze Age round cairn situated beside the minor road that links Parsley Hay and Bakewell, known locally as Back Lane. Approximately 3.5km north-east of Arbor Low, it lies on the edge of a narrow enclosed band of woodland. Unfortunately, it has no formal public access.

Bee Low was the first tomb to be excavated by Thomas Bateman in the barrow digging season of 1843. Opening the Low on the 16th June, Bateman found that it was 'impossible to excavate it in a proper manner, owing to the trees growing upon the sides'. Instead of digging his usual tunnel from the edge of the mound inwards, he was forced to sink a hole down the centre of the mound where he discovered a few fragments of human bone along with a small flint arrowhead and half a dozen horse's teeth and a cremation accompanied by a chevron-patterned Beaker.

Thomas was obviously not satisfied with this first afternoon's work as he returned to the Low for a second investigation almost eight years later on the 3rd May. The team began by extending the original tunnel further into the upturned bowl-shaped mound and soon discovered a complete skeleton 'lying on its left side with the knees drawn up, and the head to the east'. Close by lay several bronze instruments includ-

A plan of the burials found by Thomas Bateman at Bee Low (Bateman 1860)

ing two awls. A second skeleton in the crouched position, but with head facing to the south-west, was unearthed further along the tunnel. This was accompanied by a 'beautiful drinking cup' only 17cm or so tall, and ornamented with a lozenge pattern. This Beaker along with a flint knife were placed 'at the angle formed by the bending of the knees'.

A stone cist containing a pile of disarticulated bones 'carefully placed in a heap in the middle, the long bones laid parallel, and the skull put on top of the heap, with the base upward'. These excavations along with others in this century by Barry Marsden have revealed that Bee Low was in use for approximately three centuries and contained at least five burials in cists or rock cut graves and five on the old ground surface.

Other Sites close by:

Site 1 – Arbor Low (circle-henge, barrows and Gib Hill), **Site 10** – Nine Stone Close stone circle, **Site 14** – The Stanton Moor Group (five stone circles, Andle Stone, Cork Stone and numerous smaller cairns), **Site 27** – Rowtor Rocks prehistoric rock art, **Site 32** – Fin Cop hillfort, **Site 33** – Castle Ring hillfort, **Site 34** – Cratcliff Rocks hillfort, **Site 35** – Ball Cross hillfort, **Site 36** – Cranes Fort.

References and Further Reading:

J. Barnatt and K. Smith "Peak District, Landscapes through Time", English Heritage & B.T. Batsford Ltd, London (1997)

T. Bateman "Vestiges of the Antiquities of Derbyshire", London (1848)

T. Bateman "Ten Years Diggings in Celtic and Saxon Grave Hills in the Counties of Derby, Stafford and York", London (1861)

B. Marsden "The Early Barrow Diggers", Tempus Publishing Ltd, Stroud (1999)

B. Marsden "The Excavation of the Bee Low Round Cairn, Youlgreave, Derbyshire", *Antiquaries Journal*, volume 50 (1970)

Site 25

Hob Hurst's House barrow, Beeley Moor, Derbyshire

Map reference: SK287692

Access

Hob Hurst's House is an unusual Bronze Age barrow located approximately 5km south-east of Baslow on the remote area of open moorland above Harland Edge. It is located close to the track that skirts Bunker's Hill Wood, just over a kilometre north-east of Park Gate stone circle and can easily be combined with a visit to this circle.

Follow directions for Park Gate (see page 62) until coming to the prominent stile marked with Chatsworth House Estate signs. Cross this stile and follow the track ahead for several metres, then turn right onto the path leading north to Bunker's Hill Wood. Keep going until arriving at a stile after the path turns to the right and crosses a stream. Go over this stile and walk in a north-easterly direction, skirting the wood. After approximately 500m there is a path running due east, follow this for 150m and you should see Hob Hurst's House, to the south of the path. To visit Park Gate, retrace your steps back along the edge of Bunker's Hill Wood, then instead of taking the path back south, follow the track which curves across the moor to the circle in a south-south-westerly direction.

Details

The barrow is made up of a central rectangular mound, approximately 8m by 7.5m wide and just under 1m in height. A rectangular bank and ditch, the northern section of which has been damaged by a packhorse track, surround the mound. A small ring of five stones, which may originally have been thirteen, stands in the centre.

When Thomas Bateman excavated the barrow in 1853, he found a stone-lined grave containing scorched human bones and two pieces of lead ore (galena). Bateman also discovered an unusual semi-circle of small sandstone rocks surrounding these bones. This practice of 'marking off' the dead was common practice in the south of England, but very rare in this part of the world.

Comments

Hob Hurst's House has obviously been the subject of several myths and legends in recent centuries and there are various suggestions as to how it came by its name.

*The barrow of Hob Hurst's House as it looked during the Victorian period
(Bateman 1860)*

Firstly, Hob is an ancient name for the devil and there is one belief that it may be a corruption of 'Hob's First House'. In the distant past ancient monuments were often considered evil and were linked with the devil.

Another Derbyshire tradition states that 'Hob Hurst' was a kindly goblin who made his home in this barrow and gave assistance to the local community. One famous story tells of how he helped a local shoemaker by making shoes for him. However, Hob was a little over enthusiastic and made so many shoes that the cobbler ended up throwing them out of the window as fast as they were produced. Apparently there is a common Derbyshire saying that something made too quickly is done 'faster than Hob Hurst can throw shoes o' t' window'.

Lastly, according to another folklore Hob was a spirit of nature who had the ability to cause havoc especially when his land was treated badly. Local farmers often tried to appease his wrath by leaving offerings of bread and milk.

Wherever the name Hob Hurst's House came from, it just demonstrates how superstitious man became about these monuments in later centuries. For our more recent ancestors the monuments must have been very difficult to understand before the science of archaeology developed, and went some way to rationally explaining how they were constructed and what they were used for. Times were often hard and when things went wrong – crops failed, plagues raged and conflict constantly threatened – people looked for something to blame. This blame usually fell on the things they could not understand. Over the millennia, the sites gained a reputation for being 'weird' and 'unnatural' and the people who frequented them labelled likewise – at least to those who held differing beliefs.

Most of the ancient monuments in this country have been linked with the Druids at some time or another. Even in the 18th and 19th centuries they were often described as 'druidical circles'. Although the sites may have been used latterly for druidic worship, there is no evidence to prove that they were actually constructed by them. In fact, historical documents testify to the fact that the druids preferred to worship in sacred groves with oak, apple, rowan, willow, ash, beech and birch being their seven sacred trees.

According to the Roman historian, Tacitus, immediately before the revolt of the British Queen Boudicca in AD60/61, the then-governor of Britain, Suetonius Paulinus, conquered the druid stronghold of the island of Mona, (Anglesey). He launched an assault on the druids and massacred them where they stood. The sacred groves (*nemetia* in Latin) described by the historian as 'devoted to Mona's barbarous superstitions' were demolished. Evidence of these places is still apparent in the place names (e.g. Buxton is *Aquae Arnemetiae* in Latin).

The Roman historians were well known for over exaggeration, both to make their emperors and generals seem braver than they actually were and to justify their military conquests. Thus, perhaps unfairly, the druids gained a bad reputation from the Romans, particularly for their human sacrifices; yet the Romans themselves practised human sacrifice by sending innocent victims into the Arena in the name of entertainment. In later years the unknown rituals, supposedly connected with these monuments, created myths of evil, so much so that in AD567, the Church Council of Tours ruled that those who 'worshipped trees, stones or fountains should be excommunicated'.

By the Middle Ages, before science had discredited magic and tamed religion, myths and superstitions were rampant throughout Europe. When things went wrong (events that can now be explained perfectly rationally and naturally) people feared the worst and began lashing out. This whole ethos of superstitious hysteria reached a peak with the Witch Craze that spread throughout Europe in the 16th and 17th centuries. It is likely that during this period many of the ancient sites were ransacked and defiled.

By the 18th century the age of the antiquarian had dawned, when men began to look at the sites more rationally, but sadly, in many cases, caused further destruction as they excavated without proper training. Speed was of the essence with sites often dug in a single afternoon. Farmers, road builders and quarrymen accelerated their demise as they carted off the best pieces of stone for use elsewhere.

When taking all this into consideration, it is amazing sometimes that there are any prehistoric monuments left at all. Most of the sites that have survived are located on areas of high, remote moorland. Who knows how many other megaliths there may once have been, now perhaps buried under modern towns or incorporated into roads, buildings and dry-stone walls.

The folklore surrounding the circles and burial mounds is not all bad, however, and this could have aided their preservation. Other myths include the belief that the stones could bring luck to unmarried women and help them to find a husband, could boost fertility and could even cure various illnesses. Of particular benefit were stones with a hole in which people could crawl through such as the Mên-an-Tol in Cornwall. Numerous edicts passed between AD450 and AD1100 prohibiting the custom of people resorting to stone monuments for the cure of disease attest to the considerable antiquity of such beliefs.

Other Sites close by:

Site 6 – The Barbrook Group (three stone circles, a barrow, two ringcairns and numerous small cairns), **Site 11** – Park Gate stone circle, **Site 18** – Gibbet Moor North stone circle, **Site 25** – Hob Hurst's House barrow, **Site 26** – Gardom's Edge (Neolithic enclosure, barrow and prehistoric rock art), **Site 35** – Ball Cross hillfort.

References and Further Reading

W. Anthony "Haunted Derbyshire and the Peak District", Breedon Books Publishing Company, Derby (1997)

J. Barnatt "The Henges, Stone Circles and Ringcairns of the Peak District", Department of Archaeology and Prehistory, University of Sheffield (1990)

T. Bateman "Ten Years Diggings in Celtic and Saxon Grave Hills in the Counties of Derby, Stafford and York", London (1861)

B. Beare "England Myths and Legends", Parragon Books (1996)

L.V. Grinsell "The Ancient Burial Mounds of England", Methuen & Co, London (1953)

Prehistoric Rock Art

Prehistoric art is common throughout the world. Images of cave paintings such as those found in Lascaux in the Dordogne region of France, depicting animals and men hunting and gathering, adorn books and T-shirts. Britain's best-known examples of prehistoric rock art are not painted in caves, however, but carved on outcrops and crags, stone circles and cairns, across the north of the country. Here ancient man laboriously etched abstract patterns, perhaps using a hard stone tool and a mallet. Motifs include rings and hollows (cupmarks), zigzags, spirals, and arcs. Over 2500 sites are currently known, with the most southerly concentration located in Derbyshire.

Rock art is very difficult to date but as some appears in association with prehistoric monuments, it is generally considered to have been common for over 1000 years in the Late Neolithic and Early Bronze Age. Some of Britain's most famous examples include the standing stone of Long Meg near to a massive stone circle in Cumbria and Little Meg close by, both of which are covered in a series of spiral patterns and lines. In the Peak District the capstone of the cist at Barbrook II stone circle is decorated with a cup and ringmark as well as a chevron pattern.

Motifs are also occasionally found on stones in Bronze Age cairns. Some are eroded and appear to be broken off larger surfaces, suggesting they were previously decorated and reused, while others seem to have been produced specifically for certain monuments. A number of cairns contain stones with freshly decorated cup and ringmarks, mostly placed face down, and may have been gifts for the dead (Beckensall, 1999). Occasionally rock art is also found on Iron Age sites such as the hillforts of Ball Cross and Burr Tor in the Peak District, but it is likely that these stones were reused and incorporated into later structures.

Many rock art motifs are based upon the circle, one of the strongest symbols in prehistoric society as we have seen previously. The simplest and most common design is the cupmark – a circular indentation chipped into the rock. Cupmarks are found singly, as well as being randomly scattered over the rocks and incorporated into larger, more complex designs. Others have 'rings' surrounding them, reminding one of the bank and ditch of a henge, or the eyes of some strange creature. Cup and ringmarks appear in over 70 per cent of British designs. Some patterns have 'grooves' taking the form of lines, chevrons, even serpent-like trails, as at Rowtor Rocks near Birchover in Derbyshire. Spirals also occur, but these are rare in comparison to other designs.

As to what the symbols actually represented or meant to prehistoric man, we will probably never know. Over the years there have been hundreds of suggestions ranging from fertility symbols, copies of tree rings and ripples, to mixing vessels, boundary or route markers, a kind of shorthand, perhaps logos similar to today's washing instructions and road signs – or even a tattooist's shop window! (Beckensall, 1999). Some believe that the simple shapes such as cupmarks were designed to hold water and may have represented the moon, sun and stars, as most of the art on natural outcrops is found on the horizontal surfaces of earthfast boulders looking up to the sky. Zigzags and chevrons, on the other hand, may symbolise the human trance (The Independent, 1st March 1999).

Complex motifs are frequently discovered at the 'entrances' or thresholds of important areas or landscapes. These include marginal areas where prehistoric paths and camps were made and hunting and herding occurred, overlooking important river valleys and running into an area of ritual (Beckensall, 1999). These could have acted as 'sign posts' for those coming from some distance away or markers for particularly special or profitable land. One such complex design has been discovered on Gardom's Edge in Derbyshire, close to a Neolithic enclosure, where people would have come together to trade items such as axes and flint tools from many miles away.

In the Peak District, prehistoric rock art is found in areas on either side of the River Derwent and is relatively rare. There are fewer motifs than in other areas but they nevertheless have a number of interesting features. Following the trend of the British Isles in general, there is a strong coincidence of rock art within monuments and at prominent places in upland and marginal areas. No examples have so far been discovered in the valleys or on the limestone plateau, but it is possible that patterns may have been painted on rocks here as limestone is not suitable for carving and would have fractured easily (Barnatt and Reeder, 1982).

Such patterns may also have been painted or carved on wood, woven into materials and even tattooed on the skin. In 1991, a well-preserved, 5000-year-old body was discovered in a glacier in the Alps. A close inspection of Oetzi the Iceman, as he came to be known, revealed a number of interesting tattoos on his arms, legs and spine. Forensic evidence demonstrated that these had been created by rubbing a blue-tinted paste, made from charcoal, into a pattern which was pricked into the skin using a sharp instrument (Spindler, 1993).

The majority of the Peak's known carvings are found on small slabs associated with Bronze Age monuments, most of which were buried and thus preserved from weathering but fortunately found by chance. There may originally have been other carvings, though as the millstone grit in Derbyshire is softer than elsewhere these have probably been eroded away.

Where designs have survived on natural outcrops such as Gardom's Edge and Rowtor Rocks they have either been buried or sheltered by trees and vegetation.

Throughout Britain, new examples are being discovered regularly, and as a result rock art is currently the topic of much academic discussion. In order to try to understand, catalogue and preserve it a research project, funded by English Heritage, is being carried out by Professor Timothy Darvill, Head of Archaeology at Bournemouth University and Professor Peter Ucko from London University's Institute of Archaeology. The result of this research will be a gazetteer of every design in the country on CD-ROM. Computers will also be used to analyse the patterns in the hope that their meaning will be discovered (The Independent, 1st March 1999). Perhaps this will bring us one step closer to unravelling the mystery of these 5,000-year-old carvings.

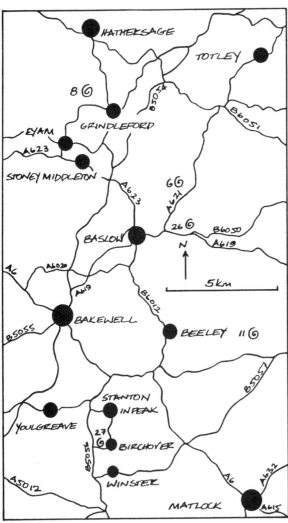

Prehistoric Rock Art in situ. Site 6: The Barbrook Group. Site 8: The Eyam Moor Group. Site 11: Park Gate stone circle. Site 26: Gardom's Edge. Site 27: Rowtor Rocks, Birchover

Site 26

Gardom's Edge, Baslow, Derbyshire

Map reference: SK272729

Access

Park in the Birchen Edge car park next to the Robin Hood pub (GR: SK281721). Walk west along the A619 for 300m and take the path to the north of the road at SK277721. Follow this in a north-westerly direction past a ringcairn, which is marked, on the map as an 'enclosure'. At SK272726, the path intersects with a wall and you should follow this wall north, ensuring you remain to the east of the southern part of the Gardom's Edge crag. Children and dogs should be kept under close supervision as there is a steep drop.

After 200m, you will come to an interesting burial cairn known as the 'Three Men of Gardom's' (GR: SK271728). Originally a Later Neolithic or Early Bronze Age barrow it now consists of three piles of stones, placed there in the 18th century, supposedly in commemoration of three shepherds who perished in the snow. Continue past this cairn for approximately 350m until you reach a stile. Having gone over the stile walk back down the line of the wall on the other side, the centre of the enclosure (a

The Three Men of Gardom's

large stone bank enclosing a boulder-strewn interior) is 100m south of the stile. The rock art is located 25m to the east of the enclosure on an earthfast rock.

Details

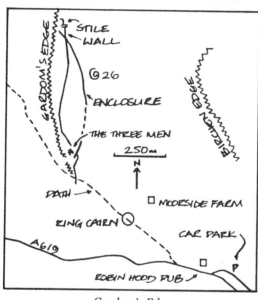

Gardom's Edge

First discovered in the 1940s when it was known as 'Meg Walls', Gardom's Edge is one of the most important archaeological sites in the Peak District. In the 1990s, this ancient landscape was surveyed by the Peak National Park Authority and the English Royal Commission and excavated by the University of Sheffield assisted by over 150 local people. These excavations unearthed an array of interesting features and showed that the site was in use for several thousand years.

The earliest construction discovered on the Edge was a huge Neolithic enclosure (GR: SK272729), originally believed to have been an Iron Age hillfort. Composed of a massive D-shaped stone bank with seven entrances, it is the first Neolithic enclosure in the uplands of Northern Britain to be surveyed in detail. The enclosed area measures an incredible 545m north/south by 150m east/west and is surrounded by a bank which varies from between 6m to 9m wide and 0.3m to 1.5m high. However, there is evidence that a considerable amount of stone has been taken, perhaps for dry-stone walls in the area, so this may account for the varying sizes.

No evidence of occupation during the Neolithic period has been found, so archaeologists believe that the enclosure, like the causewayed enclosures of southern Britain and the henge monuments of Arbor Low and the Bull Ring, may have been an important ritual and trading area. Here, artefacts such as flint arrowheads and polished axes were perhaps exchanged for crops and cattle. Lying on the main route from the Peak in the west to the flint rich areas of Yorkshire and Lincolnshire in the east, it is

The replica boulder on Gardom's Edge decorated with a series of abstract patterns

located in an ideal neutral position. Other activities carried out here may have included ritual feasting or the exposure of the dead prior to the burial of their bones.

Superimposed on the Neolithic landscape are many Later Bronze and Iron Age features including extensive prehistoric field systems, timber houses, clearance cairns and standing stones. The highlight of this sacred landscape, however, is one of the finest examples of prehistoric rock art in the Peak District. Discovered in 1965 on a large earthfast boulder 25m east of the enclosure (GR: SK273730), the design consists of a series of cup and ringmarks together with a small spiral and two circles that enclose multiple cupmarks. Unfortunately, the original boulder had to be reburied some years ago as the pattern was quickly eroding away, but an exact replica fibre glass cast now sits in its place and is well-worth seeing.

Another rock with a flattened circle containing thirteen cups was discovered during an early excavation (GR: SK275732) and can now be seen in the Sheffield City Museum.

Other Sites close by:

Site 6 – The Barbrook Group (3 stone circles, a barrow, 2 ringcairns and numerous small cairns), **Site 9** – Froggatt Edge stone circle, **Site 16** – Lawrence Field possible stone circle, **Site 11** – Park Gate stone circle, **Site 18** – Gibbet Moor North stone circle, **Site 25** – Hob Hurst's House barrow.

References and Further Reading

S. Ainsworth and J. Barnatt "A Scarp Edge Enclosure at Gardom's Edge, Baslow, Derbyshire", *DAJ*, volume 118 (1998)

J. Barnatt and K. Smith "Peak District, Landscapes through Time", English Heritage & B.T. Batsford Ltd, London (1997)

S. Beckensall "British Prehistoric Rock Art", Tempus Publishing Ltd, Stroud (1999)

J. Barnatt and P. Reeder "Prehistoric Rock Art in the Peak District", *DAJ*, volume 102 (1982)

British Archaeology, volume 23, April 1997.

Gard Web Website – www.shef.ac.uk/uni/projects/geap

R.W.B. Morris "The Prehistoric rock art of Great Britain: a survey of all sites bearing motifs more complex than simple cup-marks", *Proceedings of the Prehistoric Society*, volume 55 (1989)

Peak National Park website – www.peakdistrict.org

Site 27

Rowtor Rocks, Birchover, Derbyshire

Map reference: SK235621

Access

Rowtor Rocks is an impressive gritstone outcrop shrouded in woodland and located close to Stanton Moor to the rear of the Druid Inn in Birchover. It can be reached by parking in the village and following the track past the pub. After about 30 metres there is a path to the right-hand side (north) leading up through the trees. Please note the Druid Inn car park is reserved for patrons only. Follow this path and eventually you will come to the foot of the rocks where you can either follow the path round to the left or go up through the steps carved into the outcrop.

For those with small children, the former route is easiest. Visitors should be aware that there are several steep drops and holes in the ground.

On reaching the top of the Rocks, you will discover a large round outcrop of gritstone with a single large bench cut into it. Walking a little further, you will also find the 'armchair' – a three-seater cut into the stone. Explore and enjoy the outcrop for yourself.

Details

Rowtor Rocks, like nearby Harborough Rocks, has had a long mistaken association with the Druids. Many of the rocks are carved with a number of alcoves, rooms, caves and benches. Many of these carvings are reputed to have been made by Thomas Eyre who lived at Rowtor Hall during the 17th century. He is said to have dabbled in witchcraft, but also built the local church. The outcrop was also the site of a famous 'rocking stone' a huge boulder that moved by itself even when there was no wind blowing. This, however, was toppled by a group of boys in 1799.

Many visitors come to see the caves and modern carvings, but few actually realise that the site has been a place of great significance for thousands of years, for located at several sites around the rocks are various examples of prehistoric rock art. In all, five ancient carvings have been discovered on the western end of the outcrop with the best preserved to be found on a boulder just below the 'armchair'.

This is best found by going down between the rocks to the right of the 'armchair' when facing it, then walking back to the left (east) immediately behind the seat. There is located a large, lonesome angular boulder. The side nearest the path is only about a metre high but this rises to over two

The large boulder on Rowtor Rocks bearing three well-preserved cup and ringmarks

metres on its highest edge. The rock art, comprising three large cupmarks surrounded by single and double rings (see photos) can be found on this highest edge, at the point where the boulder drops vertically away (mind the drop). For a better view, take some water and gently pour it over the designs; this will highlight the rings better. As the boulder is under the lush, leafy canopy, the rock art is more visible in the wintertime.

Figure 5 – The carving with snake-like extension on Rowtor Rocks

The carvings are strangely etched on the very edge of the stone and at first glance look like the eyes of some strange creature such as a dragon or crocodile. The significance in placing these circles on this edge of the boulder may never be discovered; were they deliberately carved to look almost incomplete or has the boulder split fortuitously at this point?

A second rather unusual examples lies close by on a boulder a few metres further to the west on the same level as the first. The carving, which is slightly weathered, consists of a cup with a partial ring trailing off into a 'snake-like extension', a design which is unique in this area (see figure 5). A further curve (like a wing) close by makes it resemble some kind of bird.

The finest example on the rocks, however, is very unusual and lies on a small boulder approximately 5 metres down on the northern face of the

Close ups of the cup and ring marks at Rowtor Rocks

outcrop. It is composed of two concentric rings with a cross in the centre and a cupmark in each segment. Around the outside of the outer circle are a series of touching curves, resembling the petals of a flower.

Other carvings on Rowtor Rocks are said to include a couple of badly weathered simple cup and rings (one with a possible 'gutter') and numerous other cupmarks which could be man-made or could be natural. Unfortunately, we were unable to locate these examples, but for those who are interested, a reconstruction of them, and indeed all the rock art in the Peak District, can be found in volume 102 of the *Derbyshire Archaeological Journal*.

Site 10 – Nine Stone Close stone circle, **Site 14** – The Stanton Moor Group (5 stone circles, Andle Stone, Cork Stone and numerous smaller cairns), **Site 20** – Minning Low chambered round cairn, **Site 21** – Green Low chambered cairn, **Site 24** – Bee Low round cairn, **Site 33** – Castle Ring hillfort, **Site 34** – Cratcliff Rocks hillfort, **Site 36** – Cranes Fort.

Other examples of rock art in the Peak District

Included below is a brief list of rock art associated with other sites mentioned in this book.

Ball Cross (Site 35) – three sandstone stones decorated with various cup, ring and groove marks were found in the ditch of this hillfort and are now housed in the Sheffield City Museum. Of particular interest is one shaped into an equilateral triangle (see the *Defended Hilltop Sites* section for further information).

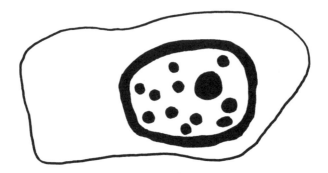

Figure 6 – The large boulder found in the ditch at Ball Cross hillfort during excavations in the 1950s

Barbrook II stone circle (Site 6) – a small stone was found under a cairn with ten cupmarks on its flat base and four lines of cups on the top (now in the Sheffield Museum); another small slab with three cups and a right-angled groove on its upper face was discovered and is still located next to the ruined cist; a kerb stone of the small internal cairn has a single cup on its upper edge.

Barbrook barrow, near Barbrook I stone circle (Site 6) – four stones decorated with various cup and ringmarks were discovered during excavations and are now housed in the Sheffield Museum store.

Burr Tor (Site 31) – a slab decorated with spirals often associated with passage graves was found somewhere near the hillfort and is now on display in Sheffield Museum.

Eyam Moor (Site 8) – Ordnance Survey maps mark a cup and ringmarked stone at SK224793, while a carving supposedly representing two deer horn tools was recorded in the 1920s on another boulder. Another possible example bearing two cupmarks can be found on one of the upright stones in the north/north-east of Wet Withens stone circle, but this may be natural.

Park Gate stone circle (Site 11) – the tallest stone has two hollows which could either be cupmarks or natural indentations.

Robin Hood's Stride near Nine Stone Close (Site 10) – a large carved ring was uncovered from vegetation in 1978 on the south-eastern side of the outcrop on a wide horizontal ledge.

References and Further Reading

J. Barnatt and P. Reeder "Prehistoric Rock Art in the Peak District", *DAJ*, volume 102 (1982)

S. Beckensall "British Prehistoric Rock Art", Tempus Publishing Ltd, Stroud (1999)

R.W.B. Morris "The Prehistoric rock art of Great Britain: a survey of all sites bearing motifs more complex than simple cup-marks", *Proceedings of the Prehistoric Society*, volume 55 (1989)

J. Stanley "An Iron Age Fort at Ball Cross", *DANHSJ*, volume 74 (1954)

Defended Hilltop Sites

During the Late Bronze Age and Early Iron Age the landscape of the British Isles changed when, due to a rising population and a deteriorating climate, communities ceased to build ritual monuments and elaborate burial tombs. Instead, they focused their attention on the defence of hilltop sites, generally referred to as 'hillforts'.

In Britain there are over 3,000 such forts, ranging from about 0.2 hectares (0.5 acres) to 320 hectares (800 acres) in size. The majority lie on hills on a level below 305m (1000ft) above sea level and are believed to have been created during a period of uncertainty and tension from around 650BC onwards. However, recent research has shown that the defence of hilltop sites has a long and varied history, occurring at different times in different places. At the beginning of the 1st millennium BC, an increased rainfall and drop in temperature had turned many areas of fertile arable land into useless blanket bog, while deforestation and continuous exploitation made the soils, even in newly colonised areas, deteriorate. This created increased pressure for food forcing communities to reorganise themselves in order to defend what agricultural land they had left. In the Peak District many of the farms on the gritstone uplands were abandoned.

Essentially, a hillfort was a heavily fortified structure, protected by a number of defences which could include earth and stone ramparts, palisade fences, ditches, specially designed entrances and natural slopes and precipices. Some appear to have been constructed as a place for temporary refuge and are almost devoid of occupation, while others were early forms of towns with buildings and food stores carefully laid out; administration, trade, industry and craft also took place on site. These hilltop sites provided the setting for ritual activity, with feasting and the sacrifice of animals, household objects and in some cases even people, taking place. Religious beliefs are also apparent in the laying out of many of these sites as roundhouses, and entrances are often orientated directly towards the equinox or midwinter solstice (Haselgrove, 1999).

Hillforts were by no means the only type of settlement in the Iron Age; there are many examples of contemporary open settlements, as well as small-enclosed farmsteads occupied by single households. After about 400BC, the climate began to improve and by the time of the first visit by the Romans to Britain it was more or less the same as it is today. In most areas hillforts were abandoned as Late Iron Age man was again able to settle on wetter, heavier soils and the pressures on the land eased. At a small number of sites, however, defences were massively extended with multiple earthworks, ditches, long entrances and complex outworks constructed.

Evidence from the Peak District bears witness to the fact that hilltop settlements and defences were not just an Iron Age phenomenon, but in some cases existed much earlier. For example, at Mam Tor and Ball Cross Bronze Age pottery fragments have been discovered, while Gardom's Edge, originally thought to be a fort, has now proved to be a Neolithic enclosure. Carl Wark and the newly discovered site at Cratcliff Rocks share many similarities with Gardom's Edge. Very little investigation has taken place on the forts of the Peak and until more work is carried out one can only speculate on their dates. It may just be the case that the hilltop sites were occupied during the Bronze Age, but defended later at the beginning of the Iron Age.

Nine examples of defended hilltop sites are known in the Peak District (excluding Gardom's Edge): Mam Tor near Castleton (SK128837), Carl Wark above Hathersage (SK259815), Castle Naze (also known as Combs Moss) above Chapel-en-le-Frith, (SK054785), Burr Tor above Great Hucklow (SK179782), Fin Cop above Ashford (SK175710), Castle Ring near Nine Stone Close stone circle (SK221628), Cratcliff Rocks on Harthill Moor (SK227623), Ball Cross above Bakewell (SK228691), and possibly Cranes Fort near Youlgreave (SK203659) – not marked on the OS map.

Most of the Peak forts have a single rampart (earthen bank) and external ditch, except Castle Naze and Fin Cop which have a double rampart, and Carl Wark which has no ditch. Nearly all are located on prominent hilltops looking down over areas which were likely to have been the main focus of settlement in the Iron Age (Barnatt & Smith, 1997). Of all those mentioned above, only Mam Tor and Carl Wark are really worth climbing.

Roundhouses reconstructed on their original postholes at Castell Henllys hillfort in Pembrokeshire give an idea of how the sites may once have looked

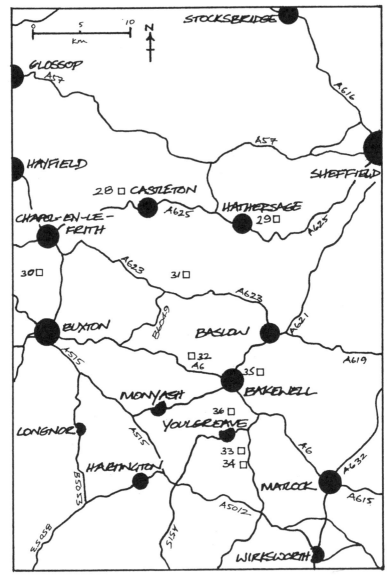

The Defended Hilltop Sites of the Peak District. Site 26: *Gardom's Edge Neolithic enclosure.* **Site 28:** *Mam Tor hillfort and barrows.* **Site 29:** *Carl Wark hillfort.* **Site 30:** *Castle Naze hillfort.* **Site 31:** *Burr Tor hillfort.* **Site 32:** *Fin Cop hillfort.* **Site 33:** *Castle Ring hillfort.* **Site 34:** *Cratcliff Rocks hillfort.* **Site 35:** *Ball Cross hillfort.* **Site 36:** *Cranes Fort hillfort*

Site 28

Mam Tor Hillfort, near Castleton, Derbyshire

Map reference: SK128837

Access

The best way to ascend the largest of the Peak's hillforts is to park in the Mam Nick car park on the Castleton to Chapel-en-le-Frith road (SK123832) and follow the steep footpath to the summit. However, for a better view of the defences, it is best to look at the Tor from a distance. One of the best places is on the B6061 (from Sparrowpit to Winnats Pass) near Oxlow House.

Details

Now in the care of the National Trust, Mam Tor, 'The Shivering Mountain', is situated above the popular tourist honey pot of Castleton, overlooking the Hope valley to the east and the Edale valley and Kinder Scout to the north. Mam Tor stands 517m (1700ft) above sea level and is part of the Lose Hill ridge; it is the only one of the large hillforts in the Peak District to have been excavated. Its eastern face is a mass of crumbling rock, below which

The view of Mam Tor from the B6061

used to lie the Castleton to Chapel-en-le-Frith road, before a landslide destroyed it in the 1970s.

Archaeological evidence indicates that the hillfort on Mam Tor began life as a partially defended site, perhaps protected by a timber palisade and ditch and developed later into a well-defended hilltop settlement with strong ramparts strengthened at the entrances. However, the remains of two Early Bronze Age barrows, which pre-date the defences, have been discovered on the summit, proving that the site must have been a focus for the local community for many years previously. These were mentioned by Thomas Bateman in 1848 when he records 'near the south-west side are two barrows, one of which was opened some years ago, and a brass celt and some fragments of an unbaked urn were found in it'. Under the care of the National Trust, one of these barrows has now been capped with stone to ensure its preservation.

The tongue-shaped earthworks, still visible today around most of the hilltop, enclose an area of approximately 5 hectares (12 acres) and consist of a single rampart, outer ditch, and a further bank, perhaps created as the ditch was cleaned out over the years. The traces of the two entrances can be seen on the paths leading from Mam Nick and Hollins Cross to the south-west and north. A stream also rises within the rampart on the north-west and flows across the line of the defences.

During excavations at Mam Tor in the 1960s, sections were cut across the ramparts to ascertain the different phases of construction. Within the interior the remains of numerous circular buildings were found, ten of which were excavated. These showed the site to be unusual in that it was constructed on sloping land with the houses terraced in platforms on the upper slopes of the hill. They appeared to date to a single period of permanent occupation. Radiocarbon dates from charcoal found on the floors of the hut platforms produced a Bronze Age date of circa 1180BC and 1130BC. These are very early for a hillfort and could perhaps relate to some form of settlement pre-dating the defensive site.

Other finds included a polished stone axe, whetstones, fragments of a shale bracelet, flints, part of a bronze axe and numerous fragments of coarse finger-moulded pottery dating to around 1000BC. Most of the pottery discovered was in the form of undecorated jars. Similar pottery was also unearthed at the Ball Cross hillfort.

Comments

Sadly the popularity of this Scheduled Ancient Monument has meant that there is a continuing erosion problem, so much so that the National Trust has had to pave the path and summit area. However, Mam Tor remains unique in the Peak District, in that it is the only one of the forts that has undergone detailed archaeological investigation. The size, position and visual impact of the fort, as well as the large amount of pottery and other artefacts yielded, make it one of the finest sites of its type in the region.

References and Further Reading

J. Barnatt and K. Smith "Peak District, Landscapes through Time", English Heritage & B.T. Batsford Ltd, London (1997)

T. Bateman "Vestiges of the Antiquities of Derbyshire", London (1848)

D.G. Coombs and F.H. Thompson "Excavation of the Hill Fort of Mam Tor, Derbyshire, 1965-69", *DAJ*, volume 99 (1979)

J. Cope "The Modern Antiquarian", Thorsons (1998)

E.J.S. Gerrish "The Prehistoric pottery from Mam Tor: Further considerations", *DAJ*, volume 103 (1983)

F.L. Preston "The Hill Forts of the Peak", *Derbyshire Archaeological & Natural History Society Journal*, volume 74 (1954)

Site 29

Carl Wark, near Hathersage, Derbyshire

Map reference: SK260815

Access

There are several ways to get to Carl Wark and it is easy to combine a visit to it with an exploration of the imposing outcrop of Higger Tor which over-looks the fortification. For the most direct route park in one of lay-bys on the Hathersage to Sheffield road near to the stile which allows you to enter the 'access land' (at GR: SK252816). From here you will find yourself 800 metres due west of the fort, so follow the path from the stile up hill until it levels out. After 100 metres there is a walled field – continue on the path past this and you will see Carl Wark immediately ahead of you with Higger Tor to the left (to the north).

Details

Described as 'amongst the most spectacular and easily accessible forts in the country', Carl Wark is located on a rocky outcrop of gritstone on Hathersage Moor, 380m (1246 ft) above sea level. The site encloses an area of about 0.8 hectares (2 acres) and is defended naturally on most sides by steep slopes. The side that is not protected by nature has seen the addition of a high rampart, constructed from earth and faced with a wall of large gritstone boulders.

In 1950, the western defences of the fort were excavated by Mr F.G. Simpson, when the interior of the rampart was found to be composed of turf. He postulated that the hillfort at Carl Wark dated from the 5th or 6th century AD because of its similarities to the Dark Age forts in southern Scotland. However, during a visit by the Prehistoric Society in 1952, a number of leading archaeologists were unconvinced by this theory, owing to the fact that the 'inturned' entrance was very similar to those at other Iron Age hillforts.

Following recent research at Gardom's Edge, it has now been suggested that Carl Wark may be another Neolithic enclosure, as the interior of this site is also very rocky with little space for buildings. As yet no finds have been discovered here, so at present it is impossible to date, but with time maybe it will prove everyone wrong and turn out to be Bronze Age!

Comments

The fort is very imposing with wonderful views across to the craggy heights of Higger Tor. The interior is strewn with many large boulders, some of

The huge stone rampart at Carl Wark

which have indentations resembling cupmarks, but are probably natural. Others have deep basin-shaped hollows which catch large amounts of rain water.

Standing on the top of the site with a cold wind blowing, it is hard to imagine why anyone would want to live in this exposed place. Times must have been hard if they were forced to retreat to such a refuge at the mercy of the elements. It is a lovely place to visit, but not an ideal habitation.

Other Sites close by:

Site 4 – Ash Cabin Flat stone circle, **Site 5** – Bamford Moor South stone circle, **Site 6** – The Barbrook Group (three stone circles, a barrow, two ringcairns and numerous small cairns), **Site 8** – The Eyam Moor Group (three stone circles and barrow), **Site 9** – Froggatt Edge stone circle, **Site 12** – Smelting Hill Stone circle, **Site 13** – Offerton Moor stone circle, **Site 16** – Lawrence Field possible stone circle, **Site 17** – Brown Edge stone circle.

References and Further Reading

S. Ainsworth and J. Barnatt "A Scarp Edge Enclosure at Gardom's Edge, Baslow, Derbyshire", *DAJ*, volume 118 (1998)

J. Barnatt and K. Smith "Peak District, Landscapes through Time", English Heritage & B.T. Batsford Ltd, London (1997)

F.L. Preston "The Hill Forts of the Peak", *DANHSJ*, volume 74 (1954)

E. Tristrum "The Promontory Forts of Derbyshire", *DAJ*, volume 33 (1911)

Site 30

Castle Naze, above Chapel-en-le-Frith, Derbyshire

Map reference: SK054785

Details

Also known as Combs Moss, Castle Naze is situated about two kilometres to the west of Dove Holes (the village famous for the Bull Ring henge) atop a steep gritstone escarpment at 427m (1400ft) above sea level. Overlooking Combs Reservoir and the village of Combs the hillfort is defended naturally on the northern and western sides and by a double rampart to the south. It can be seen from the Dove Holes to Combs road, a single-track road running to the north of the hillfort.

The fort is roughly triangular in shape, occupying approximately 0.9 hectares (2.25 acres). It was surveyed in 1957 by students from a Nottingham University summer school and The Workers' Educational Association of Buxton, when it was established that the fort had undergone three phases of construction, two of the Iron Age period and one Medieval. Obvious differences in the method of construction confirmed that the two prehistoric phases were not contemporary.

The first phase saw the construction of a dry-stone wall to the side not defended by nature, the ruins of which now survive as a grass-covered mound of rubble. These earlier defences were then replaced by a ditch with an internal bank set in front of them and a new rampart faced externally with dry-stone walling. An original causewayed entrance across the ditch was traced to the north. The third phase came much later when two 'finely engineered packhorse tracks' were constructed to ascend up through the fort.

No excavations have been carried out within the interior of the hillfort, so at the present time it is impossible to say whether it was used for permanent occupation or was just a refuge during times of trouble. The only finds, a Roman coin and Roman pottery, were discovered close to a spring which is also located inside the defences.

Other Sites close by:

Site 2 – Bull Ring henge and barrow, **Site 3** – Staden earthworks, Buxton Museum.

References and Further Reading

J. Barnatt and K. Smith "Peak District, Landscapes through Time", English Heritage & B.T. Batsford Ltd, London (1997)

F.L. Preston "The Hill Forts of the Peak", *DANHSJ*, volume 74 (1954)

H.G. Ramm "A Survey of Combs Moss Hill-Fort", *DAJ*, volume 77(1987)

E. Tristrum "The Promontory Forts of Derbyshire", *DAJ*, volume 33 (1911)

Site 31

Burr Tor, near Great Hucklow, Derbyshire

Map reference: SK179782

Details

Overlooking the limestone plateau between Eyam and Hazelbridge, Burr Tor stands at 396m (1300ft) above sea level and is also one of the region's larger hillforts. The name may derive from the Old English term *burh*, meaning a fortification. It was recognised as a hillfort as early as 1792 when a Mr Creswell of Edale noted in *Archaeologia* 'On the top of Burr Tor near Great Hucklow . . . there is an oval camp surrounded by a double ditch, not very broad or very deep. It encloses about 8 acres (I guess) by taking in the top of the Tor. It is longest from north to south . . . The entrance seems to have been at the north and south'.

In 1954, when Preston investigated the site, which is known as

A picture of Camphill, kindly supplied by the Derbyshire and Lancashire Gliding Club. The photo is taken from the south-west of the airfield (surrounded by the white perimeter track), looking north. The hillfort of Burr Tor is located in the south-west corner of the airfield.

Camphill, it was 'the landing ground of the Derbyshire and Lancashire Gliding Club'. This did (and still does) have its benefits, however, as a number of aerial photographs taken by members of the club provided a birds-eye view of the defences. The bank and ditch could be clearly traced to the east of the fort, until the ground falls away to the north-east down to Bretton Clough. On the western side, a bank and berm could be seen, while to the north a landslide had carried away the ditch, but part of the bank remained; there was no sign of the entrances, however.

Other Sites close by:

Site 8 – The Eyam Moor Group (three stone circles and barrow), **Site 12** – Smelting Hill stone circle, **Site 13** – Offerton Moor stone circle.

References and Further Reading

J. Barnatt and K. Smith "Peak District, Landscapes through Time", English Heritage & B.T. Batsford Ltd, London (1997)

F.L. Preston "The Hill Forts of the Peak", *DANHSJ*, volume 74 (1954)

Site 32

Fin Cop, near Ashford, Derbyshire

Map reference: SK175710

Details

Fin Cop hillfort is located 313m (1025ft) above sea level on a limestone crest above the village of Ashford. Drivers travelling along the A6 from Buxton to Matlock will see the hillfort in the distance as they are driving along the stretch of dual carriageway near Taddington.

The fort, enclosing an area of approximately 4 hectares (10 acres), is heavily defended by double bank and ditches to the south and east while, to the north and west, the deep gorge of Monsal Dale falls away to the River Wye below. Sadly the main site has never been excavated so nothing is known of the structures once contained within, but a further bank and ditch downslope to the south of the main rampart were investigated in the 1990s.

Discovered during a field survey of part of the parish of Ashford, the lower bank and ditch follow the line of the main earthworks, but enclose a much larger area. As the main rampart has a ditch outside and the outer embankment has a ditch inside, it has been suggested that the new earthworks are perhaps an outwork of the fort. The ground between the two may have been an area where cattle were kept to stop them straying onto lower ground. On the otherhand, it could merely be a later field boundary marker.

During the summer of 1993, a small trench was dug across the newly identified bank and ditch to try and learn more about its chronology. Excavations revealed thirteen pieces of worked flint including a scraper and a broken blade, dating to the Late Neolithic or Early Bronze Age, but it is likely that these are the remnants of earlier activity in the area. The date of both this and the main defences is still uncertain.

Other Sites close by:

Site 19 – Five Wells chambered cairn, **Site 24** – Bee Low chambered round cairn, **Site 35** – Ball Cross hillfort, **Site 36** - Cranes Fort.

References and Further Reading

J. Barnatt and K. Smith "Peak District, Landscapes through Time", English Heritage & B.T. Batsford Ltd, London (1997)

E. English and J. Wilson "Investigation of a ditch and bank at Fin Cop at Monsal Head, Ashford, Derbyshire", *DAJ*, volume 118 (1998)

F.L. Preston "The Hill Forts of the Peak", *DANHSJ*, volume 74 (1954)

Site 33

Castle Ring, near Nine Stone Close, Harthill Moor, Derbyshire

Map reference: SK221628

Details

The Castle Ring hillfort is located on a small hill at 244m (800ft) on private land behind Harthill Moor Farm, to the north-west of Nine Stone Close stone circle and near to the defended site at Cratcliff Rocks.

The fort is the smallest of those known in the region, enclosing an area of only 0.3 hectares (0.75 acres). It is oval in shape and protected by two banks and a ditch to all sides, apart from the south-east where all traces have disappeared. It was here, however, that Rooke discovered an entrance in the 18th century. He writes in *Archaeologia* in 1779, that he found the entrance 'very visible on the south-east, where part of the vallum has been levelled by the plough'.

At Castle Ring, Makepeace discovered pottery similar to that found at the Late Bronze Age or Early Iron Age settlements at Roystone Grange and Harborough rocks. He thus believes that the site may date to approximately 700BC to 500BC.

Other Sites close by:

Site 1 – Arbor Low (circle-henge, barrows and Gib Hill), **Site 10** – Nine Stone Close stone circle, **Site 14** – The Stanton Moor Group (5 stone circles, Andle Stone, Cork Stone and numerous smaller cairns), **Site 20** - Minning Low chambered round cairn, **Site 21** - Green Low chambered cairn, **Site 24** – Bee Low round cairn, **Site 27** – Rowtor Rocks prehistoric rock art, **Site 34** – Cratcliff Rocks hillfort, **Site 35** – Ball Cross hillfort, **Site 36** – Cranes Fort.

References and Further Reading

G.A. Makepeace "Cratcliff Rocks – A forgotten Hillfort on Harthill Moor, near Bakewell, Derbyshire", *DAJ*, volume 119 (1999)

F.L. Preston "The Hill Forts of the Peak", *DANHSJ*, volume 74 (1954)

Site 34

Cratcliff Rocks, Harthill Moor, Derbyshire

Map reference: SK227623

Details

The hillfort of Cratcliff Rocks lies on a gritstone promontory on Harthill Moor, close to Castle Ring and 6.5km south of Bakewell. Its identification as a hillfort was only discovered recently during a survey by G.A. Makepeace.

As at many other sites in the Peak District, the fort is defended naturally to the south and east where the land drops steeply, while to the north and west, where the land rises gently above the surrounding moor, the site is protected by a man-made construction. The fortifications include a huge wall of boulders, 55m long and 2m to 3m wide, very similar to those at Carl Wark. Elsewhere tumbled boulders may represent the remains of another wall to the west. To the north-east there appears to be an entrance. As at Carl Wark the interior is strewn with large boulders and there is little sign of domestic features.

Other Sites close by:

Site 1 – Arbor Low (circle-henge, barrows and Gib Hill), **Site 10** – Nine Stone Close stone circle, **Site 14** – The Stanton Moor Group (5 stone circles, Andle Stone, Cork Stone and numerous smaller cairns), **Site 20** - Minning Low chambered round cairn, **Site 21** - Green Low chambered cairn, **Site 24** – Bee Low round cairn, **Site 27** – Rowtor Rocks prehistoric rock art, **Site 36** – Cranes Fort.

References and Further Reading

G.A. Makepeace "Cratcliff Rocks – A forgotten Hillfort on Harthill Moor, near Bakewell, Derbyshire", *DAJ*, volume 119 (1999)

Site 35

Ball Cross, Calton Hill, near Bakewell, Derbyshire

Map reference: SK228691

Details

Ball Cross stands to the north-east of Bakewell and can be viewed from the road known locally as Handley Lane, near Ball Cross Farm. It looks across to the nearby hillforts of Fin Cop and Castle Ring.

Located on a sandstone escarpment at 259m (850ft) above sea level, the hillfort of Ball Cross is very small and encloses an area of around only 0.7 hectares (1.75 acres). It is defended by a precipitous edge on the two sides facing the valley and by horseshoe-shaped bank and ditch to the west. It was first discovered in 1821 by a London publisher whilst visiting his brother in Bakewell. The site remained untouched, however, until the 1950s, when it was excavated by Mr John Stanley with assistance from boys at Stockport Grammar School. Several trenches cut through the defences revealed that the site had undergone three phases of occupation, one prehistoric, one perhaps during the Roman period and one in the 16th century.

The most prominent features detected were the Iron Age rampart and ditch along with a strong stone wall, which appeared to have been deliberately knocked down after the first phase of occupation. A second weaker wall was located along the foundations of most of the original wall, as well as on a low bank to the south. Halfway along this bank the paved floor of a medieval building and associated pottery were discovered. This area also produced numerous fragments of coarse pottery including portions of four large cooking pots dating to around 1000BC, along with a number of querns, a jet bead and several pieces of worked flint.

Of particular interest were a number of carved stones unearthed in the ditch. The 'most exciting find' was a very large boulder 'decorated with twelve cup-like depressions enclosed in an irregular cartouche', which was lifted only with the aid of a tractor (see figure 6 on page 130). Also discovered were two further cupmarked stones, one triangular-shaped and one a broken fragment which may also have been triangular. Stanley believes at some time these could have originally stood on top of the wall. All the stones are now housed in the Sheffield City Museum.

Other Sites close by:

Site 10 – Nine Stone Close stone circle, **Site 11** – Park Gate stone circle,

Site 14 – The Stanton Moor Group (5 stone circles, Andle Stone, Cork Stone and numerous smaller cairns), **Site 18** – Gibbet Moor North stone circle, **Site 25** – Hob Hurst's House barrow, **Site 26** – Gardom's Edge (Neolithic enclosure, barrow and prehistoric rock art), **Site 32** – Fin Cop hillfort, **Site 33** – Castle Ring hillfort, **Site 36** – Cranes Fort.

References and Further Reading

F.L. Preston "The Hill Forts of the Peak", *DANHSJ*, volume 74 (1954)

J. Stanley "An Iron Age Fort at Ball Cross", *DANHSJ*, volume 74 (1954)

Site 36

Cranes Fort, Conksbury, near Youlgreave, Derbyshire

Map reference: SK203659

Details

Cranes Fort is located at Conksbury, on a long limestone ridge at 233m (764ft) above sea level, to the north-east of Meadow Place Grange Farm, almost half way between Fin Cop and Castle Ring. The possibility of a fort here was first suggested in the 1950s, but only confirmed after an investigation in 1989.

Enclosing a sub-rectangular area of just under 4 hectares (10 acres), the defences consist of a single rampart composed of limestone blocks, infilled with rubble. The fort is protected by a low wall to the north and south where the ground is naturally steep, whilst to the east and west the ramparts are more substantial. Today most of the defences are hidden under enclosure walls and the site is badly damaged following intensive stone robbing and years of ploughing in the area.

Other Sites close by:

Site 1 – Arbor Low (circle-henge, barrows and Gib Hill), **Site 10** – Nine Stone Close stone circle, **Site 14** – The Stanton Moor Group (5 stone circles, Andle Stone, Cork Stone and numerous smaller cairns), **Site 24** – Bee Low round cairn, **Site 27** – Rowtor Rocks prehistoric rock art, **Site 32** – Fin Cop hillfort, **Site 33** – Castle Ring hillfort, **Site 34** - Cratcliff Rocks hillfort.

References and Further Reading

C.R. Hart and G.A. Makepeace "Cranes Fort, Conksbury, Youlgreave, Derbyshire", *DAJ*, volume 113 (1993)

Glossary

adze A hand tool with a blade attached at right angles to a wooden handle, used for dressing timber.

antiquarian An amateur archaeologist who excavated many important monuments in the past, often hurriedly.

articulated burial A burial where all the bones of the skeleton are still joined together indicating that the person was buried whole.

barrow A man-made burial mound usually constructed from earth (but commonly from stone in the Peak District). Long barrows are typically Neolithic and round barrows usually Bronze Age.

BC Dating before the time of Christ.

Beaker burials Burials of a single crouched inhumation accompanied by a special type of decorated drinking cup, known as a beaker, and a variety of rich grave goods, common in the Early Bronze Age from c2300BC onwards.

Beaker A characteristically fine, thin-walled, well-fired drinking vessel, usually red in colour and covered with various zones of complicated geometric decoration over the majority of the exterior surface.

berm The level area between a ditch and bank.

Bluestones The famous stones at Stonehenge taken originally from the Preseli Mountains in South West Wales, so named because of their colour.

Bronze Age Dates vary according to place and culture (and the books you read), but in the British Isles it is generally accepted to encompass the period from circa 2300BC to circa 800BC with Early Bronze Age being circa 2300BC to 1800BC, Middle Bronze Age circa 1800BC to 1300BC and Late Bronze Age circa 1300BC to 800BC. These dates are only a rough guide. As to exactly when the Neolithic ended and the Bronze Age began no one is certain. In fact, it has now even been suggested that there may have been a brief 'Copper Age' in between.

cairn A mound of stones, sometimes as a result of clearing the land, but usually covering a burial. Cairns can either be circular (round cairn) or long (long cairn) in shape, or covering a tomb (chambered cairn). see also ringcairn.

cairnfield A group of cairns.

calcinated A substance which has been oxidised as a result of heating.

capstone A stone forming the roof of a burial chamber.

causewayed enclosure (also known as a causewayed camp) An Early and

Middle Neolithic roughly circular area enclosed by banks and ditches. Usually situated both in valley bottoms and on hilltops, they are believed to have been areas where trade occurred and rituals were carried out.

chambered tomb Any burial tomb with a chamber, usually constructed from stone, and dating to the Neolithic. Bones and other interments were commonly added over a long period and often brought out for ritual and ceremonial purposes.

chert A black or grey variety of quartz that resembles flint.

cinerary urn An urn in which the cremated ashes of the dead were placed.

circle-henge A later Neolithic circular earthen banked enclosure usually with an internal ditch and one or more entrances, and internal settings of stone.

cist A small rectangular grave pit, lined with stone slabs and covered with a capstone.

collared urns Containers which were used regularly after 2000BC as grave goods, either accompanying inhumations or holding cremated ashes. Used mainly by the inhabitants of the Dark Peak.

cove A Late Neolithic U-shaped structure, usually with two side stones and a back stone, often located in the centre of a stone circle or henge monument.

cremation Burnt human remains. Not surviving as ashes in the sense we know them today, but as burnt fragments of bone.

crop marks Light and dark marks in growing crops visible from the air, reflecting differences in the soil beneath. Parched lines indicate stone walls whereas greener crops grow where there is more water such as in pits, ditches and gulleys.

Cupmark A small, man-made, eggcup shaped hollow ground into stone and sometimes surrounded by a ring (ringmark). It is the most common feature in prehistoric rock art.

Dark Ages The centuries after the Roman period from cAD400, so called because the inhabitants of this time left little for archaeologists to find.

dendrochronology The use of tree rings to date ancient wooden objects.

disarticulated burial A burial with a collection of bones rather than a whole skeleton. Bodies were defleshed before burial. Usually certain bones such as the skull and long bones were placed in a tomb with those of others.

druid A Celtic priest.

dry-stone wall A wall constructed without mortar.

earthfast boulder A boulder embedded in the ground, the surface of which is visible.

earthworks Banks and ditches, mounds and hollows made from earth, clay, soil or turf.

embanked circle A stone circle set into a bank of earth or stone, characteristically rubble in Derbyshire.

enclosure Any space or area enclosed by a bank and ditch for a specific reason.

equinox The days when day and night are of equal length, exactly half way between the solstices. The vernal equinox usually occurs around the 21st March, while the autumnal equinox is around the 21st September.

excarnation platform An area where dead bodies were exposed to remove the flesh from the bones before burial. Similar practices are still carried out today in certain areas of the East.

faience beads Beads made from a glass-like material, usually found in association with Early Bronze Age burials. Common types include star-shaped and segmented varieties.

flint A very hard silica-based rock, often used for arrowheads, blades and other cutting tools, as well as lighting fires.

Food Vessel An Early Bronze Age decorated pot often found accompanying a burial.

forecourt The area of a barrow, often paved, where rituals were carried out.

Four Poster A small Bronze Age circle consisting of four stones, but not usually in a square.

grave goods Items such as pottery, tools, weapons and jewellery placed with a burial or inhumation as an accompaniment to the next world.

Grimston ware A type of Early Neolithic pottery. Dating from circa 3300BC onwards is characteristically plain, fine and hard with a round base, sometimes burnished and tempered with grit.

Grooved ware A flat-bottomed, bucket or flower-pot shaped pottery, characteristically thick and decorated with grooved lines. Dating to the Late Neolithic and Early Bronze Age (circa 3000 to 2000BC).

henge A later Neolithic circular earthen banked enclosure usually with an internal ditch and one or more entrances, which may or may not have internal settings of timber or stone.

hillfort A hilltop defended by a wall, earthen bank or timber palisade and a ditch, dating from the Late Bronze Age to Iron Age.

hoard A store of coins or other metal objects of worth, which were hidden and never reclaimed by the owner.

inhumation An uncremated human burial where the skeleton is placed either in a crouched position or lying flat.

interment The burial of a corpse, especially with ceremony.

Iron Age Most of the last millennium BC, apart from the first few hundred years, when iron became the primary metal for weapons and tools.

kerb Stones forming a retaining wall around a mound, which may be internal or external.

long barrow (see barrow)

macehead A stone tool similar to an axe head but with rounder ends.

megalithic Made from large stones.

monolith A single stone.

mortuary house A house of the dead, usually a sub-rectangular wooden structure enclosed by a bank and ditch, perhaps where bodies were exposed in order to remove the flesh before burial. Many were the starting point for barrows.

Neolithic The New Stone Age circa 4500BC to circa 2300BC with Early Neolithic being circa 4500BC to 3500BC, Middle Neolithic circa 3500BC to 2800BC and Late Neolithic circa 2800BC to 2300BC. These dates are only a rough guide. As to exactly when the Neolithic ended and the Bronze Age began no one is certain, it varies according to which book you read. In fact, it has now even been suggested that there may have been a brief 'Copper Age' in between.

orthostat A standing stone, usually part of a stone circle or other monument.

outlier A standing stone outside a circle or henge, thought to be associated with the monument and astronomical alignments.

palisade A strong fence made of stakes driven into the ground for defensive purposes.

Peterborough ware A Neolithic coarse, thick, round-bottomed pottery profusely decorated with a range of designs using stamps, combs, cord, fingers and bird bones.

portal stone A stone in the entrance of a stone circle or henge or forming the entrance to a burial chamber.

Pygmy Cup A specific type of urn dating to the Late Neolithic and Early Bronze Age. Used for funerary purposes, it may perhaps have contained incense.

pyrites A yellow mineral found in association with a number of metals, especially copper and tin.

quarry ditches Ditches quarried out using tools such as antler picks and rakes and ox shoulder blade shovels.

quern A round stone handmill used for grinding corn.

radiocarbon An archaeological dating method measuring the decay of radioactive carbon 14.

rampart The surrounding embankment of a fort, including walls and fences that are built on the bank.

recumbent stone Any stone that was either laid flat originally or has fallen over since construction.

revetted A wall or embankment faced with stones.

rill A small groove or gully eroded by water.

ringcairn A round cairn with an open space in the centre, often where human cremations were buried. Similar to an embanked stone circle, but without the standing stones.

ringmark (see cupmark)

rock cut grave Graves cut into natural rock.

Romano-British Native Britons and artefacts from the time of Roman occupation. (Roman occupation lasted from AD 43 when the Emperor Claudius invaded to the 5th Century AD when links with the Roman Empire were severed).

round barrow (see barrow)

scrapers Small flint instruments used for skinning animals and dating to the Neolithic and Bronze Age.

shards (or sherds) Broken fragments of pottery.

solstice The days of the year when the sun is at the maximum in the northern and southern hemispheres, i.e. the longest and shortest days of the year. Usually around the 21st June and the 21st December.

trilithon Consisting of two upright stones with a lintel across the top, similar to a doorway. The best known examples are at Stonehenge.

tumulus A term often used to describe a barrow or other artificial mound, the use of which is unsure.

urn A pottery vessel in which human remains are often found.

votive deposit Offerings left as a dedication at special places such as stone circles, henges or watery places.

whetstone A stone used for sharpening edged tools and knives.

wristguard A rectangular guard made from stone, wood or metal, worn on the inner side of the wrist to protect it when drawing a bow, found in both Neolithic and Bronze Age burials.

Bibliography

Adkins, Lesley & Roy – *The Handbook of British Archaeology* (Constable, London, 1982)

Ainsworth, Stuart & Barnatt, John. – "A Scarp-edge enclosure at Gardom's Edge, Baslow, Derbyshire", *Derbyshire Archaeological Journal*, volume 118 (1998)

Alcock, L. – "The henge monument of the Bull Ring, Dove Holes, Derbyshire", *Proceedings of the Prehistoric Society 16 (1950)*

Andrew, W.J. – "The Bull Ring: a stone circle at Dove Holes", *Derbyshire Archaeological Journal*, volume 27 (1905)

Anthony, Wayne – *Haunted Derbyshire and The Peak District* (The Breedon Books Publishing Company, Derby, 1997)

Barnatt, John – *Stone Circles of the Peak* (Turnstone Books, London, 1978)

Barnatt, J. and Reeder, P. – "Prehistoric Rock Art in the Peak District", *Derbyshire Archaeological Journal*, volume 102 (1982)

Barnatt, John (with assistance from A. Myers) – "Excavations at the Bull Ring Henge, Dove Holes, Derbyshire 1984-85", *Derbyshire Archaeological Journal* volume 108 (1988)

Barnatt, John – *The Henges, Stone Circles and Ringcairns of the Peak District* (Sheffield University Press, 1990)

Barnatt, John, Manley, Ray & Short, Gary – *Arbor Low a guide to the monuments* (Peak National Park Authority, 1996)

Barnatt, J. (with contributions from F.M. Chambers) – "Recent Research at Peak District Stone Circles including Restoration work at Barbrook II and Hordron Edge, and new fieldwork elsewhere", *Derbyshire Archaeological Journal*, volume 116 (1996)

Barnatt, John & Smith, Ken – *Peak District, Landscapes through Time* (English Heritage & B.T. Batsford Ltd, London, 1997)

Barnatt, John – "Taming the Land: Peak District Farming and Ritual in the Bronze Age", *Derbyshire Archaeological Journal*, volume 119 (1999)

Bateman, T. – *Vestiges of the Antiquities of Derbyshire* (London, 1848)

Bateman, T. – *Ten Years Diggings in Celtic and Saxon Grave Hills in the Counties of Derby, Stafford and York* (London, 1861)

Beare, Beryl – *England Myths and Legends* (Parragon Books Ltd, Bristol, 1996)

Beckensall, S. – *British Prehistoric Rock Art* (Tempus Publishing Ltd, Stroud 1999)

Bord, J. & C. – *Ancient Mysteries of Britain* (Paladin, 1987)

Burl, Aubrey – *A Guide to the Stone Circles of Britain, Ireland & Brittany* (Yale University Press, 1995)

Burl, Aubrey – Prehistoric Henges (Shire Publications, Princes Risborough 1997)

Burl, A. and Milligan, M. – Circles of Stone The Prehistoric Rings of Britain and Ireland (Harville Press, London 1999).

Burl, A. – The Stone Circles of Britain, Ireland and Brittany (Yale University Press, 2000)

Cope, Julian – The Modern Antiquarian (Thorsons, 1998)

Coombs, D.G. and Thompson, F.H. – "Excavation of the Hill Fort of Mam Tor, Derbyshire, 1965-69", Derbyshire Archaeological Journal, volume 99 (1979)

Crosby, Alan – A History of Cheshire (Phillimore & Co. Ltd, Chichester, 1996)

Cunliffe, Barry – Iron Age Britain (English Heritage & B.T. Batsford Ltd, London, 1995)

Darvill, Timothy – Prehistoric Britain (B.T. Batsford Ltd, London, 1987)

Dyer, J. – Ancient Britain (B.T. Batsford Ltd, London, 1990)

English, E. and Wilson, J. – "Investigation of a ditch and bank at Fin Cop at Monsal Head, Ashford, Derbyshire", Derbyshire Archaeological Journal, volume 118 (1998)

Gerrish, E.J.S. – "The Prehistoric pottery from Mam Tor: Further considerations", Derbyshire Archaeological Journal, volume 103 (1983)

Gray, H. St George – "Arbor Low Stone Circle; excavations in 1901 and 1902", Derbyshire Archaeological Journal, volume 26 (1904)

Grinsell, L.V. – The Ancient Burial Mounds of England (Methuen & Co, London, 1953)

Hart, C.R. – The North Derbyshire Archaeological Survey (North Derbyshire Archaeological Trust, Chesterfield, 1981)

Hart, C.R. and Makepeace, G.A. – "Cranes Fort, Conksbury, Youlgreave, Derbyshire", Derbyshire Archaeological Journal, volume 113 (1993)

Haselgrove, Colin – The Iron Age" in Archaeology of Britain edited by J. Hunter and I. Ralston (Routledge, London, 1999)

Hayes, Andrew – Archaeology of the British Isles (B.T. Batsford Ltd, London, 1993)

Heathcote, J.C. – "Bronze Age Cist from Gib Hill", Derbyshire Archaeological Journal, volume 61 (1940)

Heathcote, J.P. – "Excavations at barrows on Stanton Moor", Derbyshire Archaeological Journal, volume 51 (1930)

Heathcote, J.P. – "Excavations in Derbyshire during 1938 (Report by J.P. Heathcote)", Derbyshire Archaeological and Natural History Society Journal, volume 59 (1938)

Heathcote, J.P. – Excavations at Doll Tor stone circle, Stanton Moor, Derbyshire Archaeological and Natural History Society Journal, volume 60 (1939)

Heathcote, J.P. – The Nine Stones, Harthill Moor, *Derbyshire Archaeological and Natural History Society Journal*, volume 60 (1939)

Heathcote, J.P. – Excavations on Stanton Moor, *Derbyshire Archaeological and Natural History Society Journal*, volume 74 (1954)

Heathcote, J.P. – The Nine Ladies stone circle, *Derbyshire Archaeological Journal*, volume 100 (1980)

Higham, H.J. – *The Origins of Cheshire* (Manchester University Press, 1993)

Hodges, R. & Smith, K. – *Recent Developments in the Archaeology of the Peak District* (J.R. Collis Publications, Department of Archaeology and Prehistory, University of Sheffield, 1991)

Loveday, R. – "Double Entrance Henges- Routes to the Past?" in *Prehistoric Ritual and Religion*, edited by Alex Gibson and Derek Simpson (Sutton Publishing, Stroud, 1998).

Makepeace, G.A. – Cratcliff Rocks – "A forgotten Hillfort on Harthill Moor, near Bakewell, Derbyshire", *Derbyshire Archaeological Journal*, volume 119 (1999)

Manby, T.G. – "The excavation of Green Low Chambered Tomb", *Derbyshire Archaeological Journal*, volume 85 (1965)

Manby, T.G. – "Chambered Tombs of Derbyshire", *Derbyshire Archaeological and Natural History Society Journal*, volume 78 (1958)

Marsden, B. – "The re-excavation of Green Low – A Bronze Age Round Barrow on Alsop Moor, Derbyshire", *Derbyshire Archaeological Journal*, volume 83 (1963)

Marsden, B. – "The Excavation of the Bee Low Round Cairn. Youlgreave, Derbyshire", *Antiquaries Journal*, volume 50 (1970)

Marsden, B. – "Excavations at the Minning Low Chambered Cairn, (Ballidon I), Ballidon, Derbyshire", *Derbyshire Archaeological Journal*, volume 102 (1982)

Marsden, B. – *The Early Barrow Diggers* (Tempus Publishing Ltd, Stroud, 1999)

Matthews, John & Stead, Michael J. – *Landscapes of Legend A Photographic Journey Through the Secret Heart of Britain* (Blandford, London, 1997)

Mercer, Roger "Prehistory" in *Historical Atlas of Britain, Prehistoric to Medieval* edited by N. Saul (Bramley Books, Godalming, 1998)

Mitchell, John – *A Little History of Astro-Archeaology, updated and enlarged edition* (Thames & Hudson, London, 1989)

Mohen, Jean-Pierre – *Standing Stones: Stonehenge, Carnac and the world of Megaliths* (Thames & Hudson, 1999)

Morris, R.W.B. – "The Prehistoric rock art of Great Britain: a survey of all sites bearing motifs more complex than simple cup-marks", *Proceedings of the Prehistoric Society*, volume 55 (1989)

North, John – *Stonehenge, Neolithic Man & the Cosmos* (Harper Collins, 1996)

Pearson, Michael Parker – *Bronze Age Britain* (English Heritage & B.T. Batsford Ltd, London, 1993)

Pearson, Michael Parker – *The Archaeology of Death and Burial* (Sutton Publishing Ltd, Stroud 1999)

Pegge, Rev. – "Illustrations of some druidical remains in the Peak District, drawn by Hayman Rooke Esq.", *Archaeologia*, volume 7 (1785)

Pegge, Rev. – "A disquisition on the lows or barrows in the Peak of Derbyshire, particularly that capital of British monument called Arbelows", *Archaeologia*, volume 7 (1785)

Pegge, Rev. – "Observations by the Rev. Mr Pegge on Stanton Moor urns, and druidical temple", *Archaeologia*, volume 8 (1787)

Pilkington, J. – *A view of the present state of Derbyshire* (Derby, 1789)

Pitts, Mike – *Hengeworld* (Century, London, 2000)

Porter, Lindsey – *The Peak District, Pictures from the Past* (The Cromwell Press, 1994)

Preston, F.L. – "The Hillforts of the Peak", *Derbyshire Archaeological and Natural History Society Journal*, volume 74 (1954)

Ramm, H.G. – "A Survey of Combs Moss Hill-Fort", *Derbyshire Archaeological Journal*, volume 77 (1987)

Ray, Keith – "From remote times to the Bronze Age: c.500,000 BC to c.600 BC" in *Death in England An Illustrated History* edited by P.C. Jupp and C. Gittings (Manchester University Press 1999)

Rooke, H. – "An account of some druidical remains on Stanton Moor and Hartle Moor in the Peak, Derbyshire", *Archaeologia*, volume 6 (1782)

Rooke, H. – "A further account of some druidical remains in Derbyshire", *Archaeologia*, volume 7 (1785)

Rooke, H. – "Description of some druidical remains on Harborough Rocks etc. in Derbyshire", *Archaeologia*, volume 9 (1789)

Rooke, H. – unpublished notebooks (Sheffield Museum)

Sainter. J.D.- *Scientific Rambles Round Macclesfield* (Silk Press reprint, Macclesfield 1999)

Saul. N. (ed) – *Historical Atlas of Britain, Prehistoric to Medieval* (Bramley Books, Godalming, 1998)

Souden, D. – *Stonehenge, Mysteries of the Stones and Landscape* (Collins and Brown in association with English Heritage, London 1997)

Spindler, K. – *The Man in the Ice* (Weidenfield and Nicolson, London, 1993)

Stanley, J. – "An Iron Age Fort at Ball Cross", *Derbyshire Archaeological and Natural History Society Journal*, volume 74 (1954)

Storrs-Fox, W. – "Bronze Age Pottery from Stanton Moor", *Derbyshire Archaeological Journal*, volume 48/49 (1926/27)

Tacitus, P.C. – *The Annals of Imperial Rome* (Penguin Classics, London, 1989)

Tildesley, L. – "Further Excavations on Stanton Moor; report.", *Derbyshire Archaeological and Natural History Society Journal*, volume 57 (1936)

Tristrum, E. – "The stone circle known as the 'Bull Ring', at Dove Holes, and the adjoining mound", *Derbyshire Archaeological Journal*, volume 37 (1915)

Tristrum, E. – "The Promontory Forts of Derbyshire", *Derbyshire Archaeological Journal*, volume 33 (1911)

Turner, W. – "The Bull Ring Doveholes", The Leek Times, August 23rd 1902

3rd Stone – The Magazine for the New Antiquarian, Spring 1997

Ward, J. – "Cinerary Urns and incense cups, Stanton Moor, Derbyshire", *Derbyshire Archaeological Journal*, volume 13 (1891)

Ward, Rev. R. – *A guide to the Peak of Derbyshire* (1827)

Williams, G. – *Strong Hold Britain Four Thousand Years of British Fortifications* (Sutton Publishing, Stroud, 1999)

Wilson, W. & English, E. – "Investigations of a ditch and bank at Fin Cop at Monsall Head, Ashford, Derbyshire", *Derbyshire Archaeological Journal*, volume 118 (1998)

Wood, W. – *History and Antiquities of Eyam* (1842 & 1846 – fourth edition)

Wroe, P. – "Roman Roads in the Peak District", *Derbyshire Archaeological Journal*, volume 102 (1982)

Websites of Interest

Megalithic Mysteries – www.megalithic.co.uk

A superb photographic guide to ancient sites by Andy Burnham including links to 'The Megalith Map' (www.megalith.ukf.net) allowing you to find any stone circle in England, Scotland, Wales, Ireland and the Channel Islands; the 'stone circle shop' and hundreds of similar megalithic sites on the 'Stone Circle Webring'.

Alastair's Derbyshire Stone Circle Pages –
www.geocities.com/Athens/Parthenon/6197/derbys.htm

An excellent guide to the stone circles of Derbyshire and beyond.

Ancient Sites Directory – www.henge.demon.co.uk

A guide to the Ancient Monuments of the UK

Gard Web – www.shef.ac.uk/uni/projects/geap

Website run by the Archaeology Service of the Peak District National Park Authority and the Department of Archaeology and Prehistory at Sheffield University, detailing archaeological excavations on Gardom's Edge.

Derbyshire Archaeological Society – www.nottingham.ac.uk/~aczsjm/das/

Includes details of membership to the Society as well as a list of publications including the *Derbyshire Archaeological Journal*. It also allows you to search the *DAJ* index on-line.

Peak National Park – www.peakdistrict.org

3rd Stone Magazine – www.thirdstone.demon.co.uk

All the latest news from 3rd Stone magazine, the journal of archaeology, folklore and myth

Current Archaeology Magazine – www.archaeology.co.uk

Council for British Archaeology – www.britarch.ac.uk

Useful Addresses

Buxton Museum & Art Gallery
Terrace Road, Buxton, Derbyshire, SK17 2TP
Tel: 01298 24658

English Heritage
General enquiries: Customer Services Department, PO Box S69, Swindon SN2 2YP. Tel: 0870 3331181

Peak District National Park Authority
Aldern House, Baslow Road, Bakewell,Derbyshire, DE45 1AE
Tel: 01629 816200

Sheffield City Museum
Weston Park, Sheffield, South Yorkshire, S10 2TP
Tel: 0114 276 8588

Index

Also from Sigma Leisure:

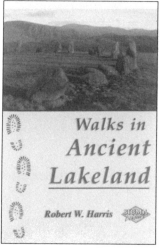

WALKS IN ANCIENT LAKELAND
Robert Harris

Enjoy a 'Walk in Ancient Lakeland' and discover sites and monuments from the Neolithic and Bronze Ages you never knew existed. Discover the great stone circles, standing stones and burial cairns which still decorate these beautiful hills. Follow the ancient trackways linking these ancient sites and explore largely unknown areas to uncover the mysteries of the lives of our ancestors in this timeless landscape.

At the same time feast your eyes over the beautiful and fascinating wild flowers and bird life which abound, in sites well away from the busier tourist areas of the ever-popular Lake District.

The author's own intricate hand-drawn sketches add to the appeal, depicting the many standing stones and circles raised in the past by our Lake District ancestors. *£7.95*

ROCKY RAMBLES IN THE PEAK DISTRICT: Geology Beneath Your Feet
Fred Broadhurst

You don't have to be an expert or even an amateur geologist to enjoy these 'rocky rambles'! Where better than in and around the Peak District would you find geology right there beneath your feet - all you need to know is where to look.

Take geology in your hands and read the colourful descriptions of the fascinating walks available in this area. Many of them are circular, varying in length (half day or full day) and aimed at ramblers interested in the rocks (their composition, structure and origin) as well as Derbyshire's incomparable scenery.

Detailed maps are included plus information about parking facilities, and the all-important venues for refreshments along the way. *£7.95*

All of our books are available through booksellers. In case of difficulty, or for a free catalogue, please contact:

SIGMA LEISURE, 1 SOUTH OAK LANE, WILMSLOW, CHESHIRE SK9 6AR.
Phone: 01625-531035   Fax: 01625-536800.   E-mail: info@sigmapress.co.uk
Web site: http//www.sigmapress.co.uk

MASTERCARD and VISA orders welcome.